TWENTIETH CENTURY VIEWS

The aim of this series is to present the best in contemporary critical opinion on major authors, providing a twentieth century perspective on their changing status in an era of profound revaluation.

Maynard Mack, *Series Editor*
Yale University

SCIENCE FICTION

SCIENCE FICTION

A COLLECTION OF CRITICAL ESSAYS

Edited by

Mark Rose

Prentice-Hall, Inc.  *Englewood Cliffs, N.J.*

Library of Congress Cataloging in Publication Data

Main entry under title:
SCIENCE FICTION.

(A Spectrum Book)
Bibliography: p.
CONTENTS: Rose, M.–Introduction.–Backgrounds:
Amis, K.–Starting points. Conquest, R.–Science
fiction and literature. Scholes, R.–The roots
of science fiction.–Theory: Suvin, D. [etc.]
1.–Science fiction—History and criticism—
Addresses, essays, lectures. I.–Rose, Mark.
PN3448.S45S27   809.3'8'76   76–19008
ISBN 0–13–794966–9
ISBN 0–13–794958–8 pbk.

Acknowledgment is gratefully made to Macmillan Publishing Co., Inc. and A.
P. Watt & Son Ltd. for permission to reprint the short excerpt from *Collected Poems*
by William Butler Yeats. Copyright © 1956 by Macmillan Publishing Co., Inc.

10 9 8 7 6 5 4 3 2 1

PRENTICE-HALL INTERNATIONAL INC. (*London*)
PRENTICE-HALL OF AUSTRALIA, PTY., LTD. (*Sydney*)
PRENTICE-HALL OF CANADA, LTD. (*Toronto*)
PRENTICE-HALL OF INDIA PRIVATE LIMITED (*New Delhi*)
PRENTICE-HALL OF JAPAN, INC. (*Tokyo*)
PRENTICE-HALL OF SOUTHEAST ASIA PTE. LTD. (*Singapore*)

To Linda and Bo, Anne and Jessica

Contents

SCIENCE FICTION

Introduction

by Mark Rose

The last decade or so has seen a shift in literary taste away from the meticulous psychological realism of, say, *Goodbye Columbus* to the brilliant extravagances of *Portnoy's Complaint*. The novels of Barth, Heller, Pynchon, and Vonnegut are symptomatic of this shift, as is the popularity of Tolkien's epic fantasy, *The Lord of the Rings*. Even so conservative a group as Renaissance scholars has felt the effects of the shift in taste as the intense critical interest in Spenser's *Faerie Queene* and Shakespeare's late romances, *The Winter's Tale* and *The Tempest*, bears witness. Most people have a healthy love of wonder and melodrama, but for many years the accepted canons of taste, committed to rather narrow ideals of realism and an Arnoldian conception of "high seriousness," rejected the basic stuff of romance as childish. Now, however, it has become possible for serious critics to reexamine areas of literature that formerly were ignored, and science fiction, which is perhaps the characteristic romance form of the scientific age, has been "discovered."

We do not expect romances to provide subtle psychological portraits or fully rendered images of the world as we know it. Rather, we expect to hear of marvels and adventures in strange places populated by such preternatural creatures as giants and dragons. The essential aesthetic effect of romance is wonder, and we have only to consider the titles of some of the science-fiction magazines such as *Amazing Stories, Thrilling Wonder Stories*, or *Astounding Science Fiction* to perceive how strongly the old hunger for the marvelous persists. Call your magic a "space warp" or a "matter transformer," your enchanted island the planet Einstein—named, of course, for that quaint twentieth-century physicist who thought it impossible to travel faster than light—call your giants and dragons "extraterrestrials," and what you have is merely the contemporary form of one of the most ancient literary kinds.

An understanding that science fiction is a romance form is perhaps the necessary prerequisite to serious discussion of the genre, for science fiction is rooted in such romance traditions as the imaginary voyage—*Gulliver's Travels* is perhaps the most familiar of these in English—and it clearly will not do to consider works of this sort in the same terms as psychological novels.[1] Romance, as a rule, moves freely toward symbolism and allegory, a tendency that contributes to one of its major literary strengths, the ability to treat broad and often explicitly philosophical issues in fictional form. In the preface to *Frankenstein*, the gothic romance which many would claim as the first science-fiction novel, Mary Shelley explains that she is not interested in merely "weaving a series of supernatural terrors" but has chosen to write a special kind of fantastic tale, one that "affords a point of view to the imagination for the delineating of human passions more comprehensive and commanding than any which the ordinary relations of existing events can yield." A more "comprehensive and commanding" point of view than can be achieved by a narrative of existing events—this is what science fiction typically seeks, and it generally achieves it by one or another of the literary strategies of what Darko Suvin, in his important essay in this volume, calls "estrangement." The science-fiction writer may, in the fashion of Mary Shelley, provide us with an analytic image of our world, as, say, Karel Čapek does in *R.U.R.*, where the tendency of an industrial society to transform people into machines is literally realized in the manufacture of human machines. Alternatively, he may provide us with some form of uncommon perspective on our world, perhaps by projecting the story into the future so that our own time is seen in a broader context than is usual or perhaps by allowing us to view ourselves from the point of view of, say, the supermen of W. Olaf Stapledon's *Odd John* or the aliens of Robert Sheckley's "Specialist." Science fiction shares the generic ability of romance to treat large themes, and from H. G. Wells's early cosmological tales such as *The Time Machine* and *The War of the Worlds* to Stanislaw Lem's epistemological fable, *Solaris*, it

[1] For discussions of romance which are particularly applicable to science fiction see Richard Chase, *The American Novel and Its Tradition* (Garden City, N.Y.: Doubleday & Company, Inc., Anchor Press, 1957), especially chapter 1, and Northrop Frye, *Anatomy of Criticism* (Princeton, N.J.: Princeton University Press, 1957), especially pp. 186–206, "The Mythos of Summer: Romance."

has been one of the few contemporary fictional forms that can deal directly with broad philosophical issues.

Being a generalizing mode, romance tends to use representative rather than individualized characters—the knight versus the evil magician or, in science fiction, the scientist versus the religious fanatic—and such matters as depth and consistency of character portrayal are normally beside the point. If the narrative follows the quest romance pattern, as most science-fiction stories do, then the figures in the tale tend to be characterized principally by their ideological relationship to the quest. Put simply, characters are either for or against the quest: the "good" or "enlightened" assist it, the "bad" or "ignorant" obstruct it. In reading a science-fiction story, then, we want to watch less for "psychology" than for the way various character types are organized in a configuration that is ultimately an expression of values. To choose a simple example, in "Universe," Robert Heinlein's story of a starship gone astray, the object of the quest is "truth," conceived as a materialistic perception of the natural world. Generations have passed since the starship's launching and the benighted descendants of the original crew have come to believe that their ship is the universe and that such notions as the "Trip" are to be understood in a religious sense. The conflict in the story is a struggle between the ship's ruling priestly class—called, ironically, "scientists"—and the more open-minded hero who makes his way to the long-forgotten "Main Control Room" where he discovers the stars and recognizes that the universe is vaster than anyone had supposed. Heinlein's "Universe" asserts materialistic against religious values, and yet the crucial revelation of the stars is presented less as a moment of cool intellectual triumph than one of quasi-religious ecstasy. There is perhaps a contradiction here between the story's asserted values and the emotional response it attempts to evoke, but, if so, it is a contradiction that is commonplace in science fiction, which repeatedly strives for just such a quasi-religious mood of awe, and perhaps it helps to explain the appeal of science fiction to an age that is fundamentally materialistic in ethos and yet not without a hunger for religious emotion.

The starry epiphany in "Universe" is a particularly clear example of the general tendency of science-fiction stories to move toward moments of apocalyptic revelation, either ecstatic or, perhaps more frequently, horrific, as befits a genre strongly influenced by the gothic novel. In Isaac Asimov's "Nightfall," for instance, a very similar revelation of the stars brings universal madness and the collapse of civilization: here the indifferent splendor of the cosmos is pictured as too terrible for the human mind to absorb. Revelations such as these, striking moments in which the transcendent and the mundane interpenetrate, are another element which associates science fiction with the romance tradition, where such epiphanies as Redcross's vision of the New Jerusalem in Book I of *The Faerie Queene* are frequent. The ability of romance to embrace the transcendent made it a suitable vehicle for religious expression in an earlier period. And perhaps, as Robert Scholes notes below in "The Roots of Science Fiction," we should not be too surprised to find science fiction employing the same vehicle as religion, for science, too, emphasizes that there is more to the world than meets the eye. Telescopes, microscopes, even chalk on blackboard—these are instruments of prophecy of the unseen and sometimes unseeable worlds upon which scientific knowledge is founded.

Probably the chief interest in Heinlein's "Universe" comes less from the epiphany or even from the plot than from the setting, the description of the little universe of the ship. In realistic fiction, setting tends to be primarily a context for the portrayal of character; in romance forms, setting typically receives much more emphasis. Indeed, sometimes the setting of a romance will be more "alive," will have more "personality," than any of the characters. In *The Faerie Queene*, for instance, the most memorable and often the most dramatic parts of the poem tend to be the descriptions of such crucial locales as Lucifera's palace in Book I or the Garden of Adonis in Book III. The phenomenon of *landscape as hero* is particularly common in science fiction, where the truly active element of the story is frequently neither character nor plot but the world the writer creates, as in Hal Clement's description of "Mesklin," the imaginary Jovian-type planet of *Mission of Gravity.* Indeed, sometimes in science fiction the setting literally comes alive, as in Arthur Clarke's *Rendezvous with Rama*, where the mysteriously empty spaceship which the human protagonists are investigating suddenly begins to produce "biological robots." Frequently the settings in science-fiction stories are literal—an allegorical reading of Clement's "Mesklin" would merely be silly—but sometimes science-fictional settings do tend toward the symbolic, as in "Universe," where the starship is interesting both in its own right and as a metaphor for our world.[2]

Appreciation of the fact that science fiction is a romance form is necessary to prevent certain fundamentally improper expectations of the genre, but it alone does not provide a simple "key" to criticism. In the discussion of science fiction as of any other kind of literature there is finally no substitute for sensitivity and critical tact. Moreover, that science fiction is a form of romance should not blind us to the authentically scientific aspect of the genre. Science fiction varies in quality and in particular cases it is often impossible to distinguish from fantasy; nevertheless, the scientific element has been important from the beginning. The ivory and crystal gadget that launches H. G. Wells's time traveler into the future is magical flim-flam, but the romance itself is a meditation upon some of the human implications of Darwin's discoveries. Superficially, *The Time Machine* may be unscientific, but the fiction as a whole is informed with a scientific vision.

A great deal of science fiction is of course dependent upon flim-flam, and I implied earlier that there is little difference between magic of the sort that we get in medieval romances and such science-fictional marvels as "space warps" and "matter transformers." Let us note now, however, that in the old romances, as in modern fantasy, no explanations are required for the introduction of marvels: knights simply encounter magicians as little girls fall down rabbit holes without authorial apologies. In such worlds the marvelous is normal. Science fiction differs from fantasy in the kind of rhetoric it evokes to justify its marvels—H. G. Wells called this rhetoric "scientific patter"—and the difference in rhetoric is significant, for the scientific patter contains an implicit assertion of the truth of the scientific world view and an assurance

---

[2] This tendency to emphasize landscape helps to explain the facility with which science-fiction stories have been adapted to film, a visual medium that by its very nature also emphasizes setting. The appeal of Stanley Kubrick and Arthur Clarke's *2001: A Space Odyssey*, for instance, is obviously one of landscape, of such visual sequences as that of the space shuttle slowly aligning itself with the rotating space station while the soundtrack, playing the "Blue Danube," provides us with an aesthetic attitude toward a world of dancing, half-living machines.

that, while the laws of the cosmos may not be fully understood, still there are laws.

In the "Preface to Lyrical Ballads," written only a few years before *Frankenstein*, Wordsworth makes a statement that looks forward to a great deal of science fiction:

> If the labors of men of science should ever create any material revolution, direct or indirect, in our condition, and in the impressions which we habitually receive, the poet will sleep then no more than at present; he will be ready to follow the steps of the man of science, not only in those general indirect effects, but he will be at his side, carrying sensation into the midst of the objects of the science itself. The remotest discoveries of the chemist, the botanist, or mineralogist will be as proper objects of the poet's art as any upon which it can be employed, if the time should ever come when these things shall be familiar to us, and the relations under which they are contemplated by the followers of these respective sciences shall be manifestly and palpably material to us as enjoying and suffering beings. If the time should ever come when what is now called science, thus familiarized to men, shall be ready to put on, as it were, a form of flesh and blood, the poet will lend his divine spirit to aid the transfiguration, and will welcome the being thus produced, as a dear and genuine inmate of the household of man.

Science fiction, contrary perhaps to popular opinion, is rather poor as an instrument of scientific prediction, but it is an excellent medium for the exploration of the taste, the feel, the human meaning of scientific discoveries. There is, for example, a category of stories concerned with microscopic worlds. These tales, which were more popular some years ago than they are today, are generally little more than adventure stories in the exotic settings provided by the microscopic landscapes. As a class they tend to be one of the less interesting varieties of science fiction. Nevertheless, even in this category we can detect an attempt to come to grips with the still stunning discovery that there is a world of life in every drop of water. Indeed, the very image of a miniaturized man in a microscopic landscape—James Blish's "Surface Tension" or Isaac Asimov's *Fantastic Voyage* will do for examples—can be appreciated as a symbol of the attempt to make this world more than a scientific fact but part of human experience.

If the critical discovery of science fiction can be understood as part of a change in our literary sensibility that has led to a renewal of interest in romance forms, it must also be seen as part of the general rise of interest in uncanonical cultural forms such as popular and ethnic literature, a phenomenon directly associated with the social upheavals of the 1960s and 70s. Some science fiction is not popular literature. I am thinking in particular of the literate British tradition that springs from H. G. Wells and includes such writers as W. Olaf Stapledon, C. S. Lewis, and Aldous Huxley. But the bulk of American science fiction, especially that published in the heyday of the science-fiction magazines, *is* popular literature. Recently, however, science fiction has begun to spawn writers who employ the themes and conventions of the rather provincial popular tradition with a literary sophistication equal to that of almost anyone writing today, and in connection with these writers the very concept of "high" versus "popular" culture seems beside the point.

The appearance of such authors as Stanislaw Lem and Ursula K. LeGuin—to cite only two of the most notable current writers—has occurred simultaneously with the rise of critical interest in science fiction. Indeed, some of the new science-fiction writers have themselves produced notable works of criticism. If science fiction has until recently been rather provincial, so too has criticism in its conception of literature and of the kinds of material that constitute appropriate subjects for critical inquiry. Both science fiction and criticism have been changing rapidly, however, and now, as the essays in the present volume indicate, critics and authors together have at last begun a sustained exploration of the literary possibilities inherent in the genre.

PART ONE

Backgrounds

Starting Points

by Kingsley Amis

Those who have never seen a living Martian can scarcely imagine
the strange horror of its appearance. The peculiar V-shaped mouth
with its pointed upper lip, the absence of brow ridges, the absence of
a chin beneath the wedge-like lower lip, the incessant quivering of
this mouth, the Gorgon groups of tentacles, the tumultuous breathing of the lungs in a strange atmosphere, the evident heaviness and
painfulness of movement due to the greater gravitational energy of
the earth—above all, the extraordinary intensity of the immense
eyes—were at once vital, intense, inhuman, crippled and monstrous.
There was something fungoid in the oily brown skin, something in
the clumsy deliberation of the tedious movements unspeakably
nasty. Even at this first encounter, this first glimpse, I was overcome
with disgust and dread.

If that produces no special reaction—it comes, of course, from an
early chapter of *The War of the Worlds*—perhaps this passage will:

"I don't have to tell you men that Point-of-Sale has its special
problems," Harvey said, puffing his thin cheeks. "I swear, the whole
damned Government must be infiltrated with [Conservationists]!
You know what they've done. They outlawed compulsive subsonics
in our aural advertising—but we've bounced back with a list of
semantic cue words that tie in with every basic trauma and neurosis
in American life today. They listened to the safety cranks and
stopped us from projecting our message on aircar windows—but we
bounced back. Lab tells me," he nodded to our Director of Research
across the table, "that soon we'll be testing a system that projects
direct on the retina of the eye...." He broke off, "Excuse me, Mr.
Schocken," he whispered. "Has Security checked this room?"

Fowler Schocken nodded. "Absolutely clean. Nothing but the

"Starting Points." From Kingsley Amis, *New Maps of Hell: A Survey of Science
Fiction* (New York: Harcourt, Brace and Company, 1960), pp. 15–41. Copyright ©
1960 by Kingsley Amis. Reprinted by permission of Harcourt Brace Jovanovich,
Inc. and A D Peters & Co Ltd.

usual State Department and House of Representatives spymikes. And of course we're feeding a canned playback into them."

I quote that extract from *The Space Merchants* (a novel published in 1953) and the H. G. Wells piece in order to make possible a tiny experiment in self-analysis: anybody encountering such passages who fails to experience a peculiar interest, related to, but distinct from, ordinary literary interest, will never be an addict of science fiction. Now I acknowledge that people can live out happy and useful lives in complete indifference to this form of writing, but the point about addiction is the one where investigation should start. Those who decide that they ought to "find out about" science fiction, suspecting that it furnishes a new vantage point from which to survey "our culture," will find much to confirm that suspicion and also, I hope, much incidental entertainment, but they are unlikely to be able to share, nor even perhaps to comprehend, the experience of the addicts, who form the overwhelming majority of science-fiction readers, and to whom, naturally, entertainment is not incidental but essential. As is the way with addictions, this one is mostly contracted in adolescence or not at all, like addiction to jazz. The two have much in common, and their actual coexistence in the same person is not unusual.

The two modes themselves, indeed, show marked similarities. Both emerged as self-contained entities some time in the second or third decade of the century, and both, far more precisely, underwent rapid internal change around 1940. Both have strong connections with what I might call mass culture without being, as I hope to show in the case of science fiction, mass media in themselves. Both are characteristically American* products with a large audience and a growing band of practitioners in Western Europe, excluding the Iberian peninsula and, probably, Ireland. Both in their different ways have a noticeably radical tinge,

* The prehistory of science fiction, up until 1914 or later, is admittedly as much British as American, and until quite recently the phenomenon of the serious author who takes an occasional trip into science fiction (Huxley, Orwell, William Golding—in a rather different sense) has been British rather than American. But the general run is so firmly American that British science-fiction writers will often fabricate American backgrounds and fill their dialogue with what they believe to be American idioms. (Compare the British "tough" thriller, at any rate on its lower levels.)

showing itself again and again in the content of science fiction, while as regards jazz, whose material is perforce non-political, radicalism of some sort often appears in the attitudes of those connected with it; a recent article in the *Spectator* claimed that one might as well give up hope of meeting a British intellectual committed to jazz who was not firmly over to the left in politics. Both of these fields, again, have thrown up a large number of interesting and competent figures without producing anybody of first-rate importance; both have arrived at a state of anxious and largely naïve self-consciousness; both, having decisively and for something like half a century separated themselves from the main streams of serious music and serious literature, show signs of bending back towards those streams. One shouldn't go on like this all night; the two forms have no helpful resemblance, for example, in origin or in role, but I should like to round off this catalogue of supposed parallels by observing that both jazz and science fiction have in the last dozen years begun to attract the attention of the cultural diagnostician, or trend-hound, who becomes interested in them not for or as themselves, but for the light they can be made to throw on some other thing. By saying this I mean only to distinguish this interest, not to denigrate it; it seems worthy enough, even praiseworthy.

A definition of science fiction, though attempted with enormous and significant frequency by commentators inside the field, is bound to be cumbersome rather than memorable. With the "fiction" part we are on reasonably secure ground; the "science" part raises several kinds of difficulty, one of which is that science fiction is not necessarily fiction about science or scientists, nor is science necessarily important in it. Prolonged cogitation, however, would lead one to something like this: Science fiction is that class of prose narrative treating of a situation that could not arise in the world we know, but which is hypothesised on the basis of some innovation in science or technology, or pseudo-science or pseudo-technology, whether human or extra-terrestrial in origin. This is the kind of definition that demands footnotes. "Prose narrative," then, because the appearance of science-fiction interests in verse form have so far been of minor extent. An occasional dreadful poem about the majesty of the stars and so on struggles into one or another of the magazines as a page-filler, and there is in England a

poet of some standing, Robert Conquest, whose works include an
ode to the first explorers of Mars and a report on Terran culture
imagined as the work of a survey team constituted by the
headquarters of the Galactic Federation (plus a whole science-
fiction novel, *A World of Difference*). But Conquest is at the moment a
rather lonely figure, or perhaps a pioneer. I draw attention also to
the existence of a volume called *The Space Child's Mother Goose*, which
contains ingenious, but not always striking, variations on nursery
rhymes—"This is the theory that Jack built," and so on—with
contemporary *art-nouveau* illustrations. The work falls into that
category of adults' children's books which has so far unaccountably
eluded the trend-hounds (unless I have missed something, which I
well may), and although the volume got a review in *Astounding
Science Fiction*, rather puzzled in tone, I doubt if it has much
circulation among ordinary readers of that journal.

To hark back now to my definition: its crucial point, clearly, lies
in the mention of science and technology and their pseudo-forms.
Many stories are based on, or incidentally involve, perfectly
plausible extensions of existing theories and techniques. The use of
robots, for instance, still a very popular subject, seems actually
foreseeable, however unlikely, and even if the problem of fitting all
that machinery into a container on the human scale would require
the development of a kind of micro-electronics that for the time
being, one would imagine, is at a rudimentary stage. Stories based
on, or involving, space flight, again, which form probably the
largest class, can rest on principles and processes that do no violence
to what is already established. But those writers who feel constricted
by a mere solar system face a certain inconvenience when they set
about taking their characters to the farther parts of our galaxy or to
other galaxies. The fact is—and I apologize to all those for whom it
is an odiously familiar fact—that to reach any but the nearest stars
would take several hundred years even if one travelled at the speed
of light, in the course of doing which one would, if I understand
Einstein's popularisers correctly, become infinite in mass and zero
in volume, and this is felt to be undesirable. A few writers simply
accept this difficulty and arrange for their travellers to put
themselves into some sort of deep-freeze until just before planetfall,
or allow them to breed in captivity for the requisite number of
generations, in which case the plot will concern what happens when

a couple of centuries have elapsed and nobody on board is any longer aware of the situation. But most commonly, the author will fabricate a way of getting around Einstein, or even of sailing straight through him: a device known typically as the space-warp or the hyper-drive will make its appearance, though without any more ceremony than "He applied the space-warp," or "He threw the ship into hyper-drive." Such reticence may baffle and annoy the neophyte, as unfamiliar conventions will, but one would not demand that every Western include an exposition of ranching theory, and the space-warp is an equally acceptable convention, resting as it does on the notion that while there is a theoretical limit to the speed at which matter can be moved through space, there is no such limit to the speed at which space can be moved through space. Therefore, if the space being moved contains a space-ship, this can be shifted from the neighbourhood of the Earth to the neighbourhood of the Dog Star in an afternoon or so without any glaring affront to Einstein.

So much for real or good-imitation science; a few words now on the flagrantly pseudo variety. If aliens are to be introduced—alien is the term applied in the trade to any intelligent creature originating outside the Earth—the problem of communicating with them is likely to arise. Some excellent stories have been written about non-communicating aliens, from *The War of the Worlds* onwards, but their potentialities hardly extend beyond simple menace, and, as we shall see, recent science fiction has tended to lose interest in menace of this kind. Talking to an alien, however, presents difficulties that are literally insurmountable. One doesn't want to start too far back, but granted that communication, whatever it is, can be conceived of in other than human terms, and granted that it might involve something analogous to speech, one is still faced with a choice of infeasibilities. Direct learning of an alien language as one might under adverse conditions learn a human language, by ostensive definition and the like, entails presupposing an alien culture with human linguistic habits, which seems unlikely. The idea of a translation machine, recalling the space-warp in being usually introduced by phrases like "He set up the translation machine," differs from the space-warp in presenting a direct affront to common sense, for such a machine would clearly be foiled even by an utterance in Portuguese unless it had been "taught"

Portuguese to start with. Telepathy—"The thought-forms of the alien flooded into his mind"—cannot exist. (Or can it? According to the director of its newly formed Astronautics Institute, the Westinghouse Electric Corporation is conducting research into telepathy as a means of long-distance communication.) My concern at the moment, however, is not that all these notions are, or may be, implausible, but that they are offered as plausible and that efforts are made to conceal their implausibility. The same is true of other traditional devices: time travel, for instance, is inconceivable, but if an apparatus of pseudo-logic is not actually set up to support it, the possibility of recourse to such an apparatus will not be explicitly ruled out. The science-fiction writer works by minimising what is self-contradictory.

Whether or not an individual story does justice to the laws of nature is a consideration that can affect our judgment of it, but my purpose here is to insist that such justice is always an aim—in the field of science fiction. The point of this is that immediately adjacent to this field, and in some instances to be distinguished from it only with difficulty, lies the field of fantasy. Fantasy of the kind I am going to discuss has developed into a self-contained form of writing in the same sense and over much the same period as science fiction: the two modes appeal to some of the same interests, share some of the same readership and unite in the name of a periodical, *The Magazine of Fantasy and Science Fiction*. It will be seen that I am using the term "fantasy" in a special and restricted sense, corresponding to a special kind of publication abutting upon my subject; I am aware of the existence of a body of work that can be called fantasy, from *Beowulf* to Kafka, which anticipates and parallels this kind of fantasy in a way that nothing quite anticipates or parallels science fiction, but my business is not with that. However, I acknowledge the fact that fantasy, in the special sense, gives, despite its much smaller volume, as valid a glimpse of contemporary attitudes as does science fiction. But I think it better to say straight out that I do not like fantasy, whether from *Beowulf* to Kafka, or in the specialised contemporary magazines, rather than take the trouble of devising reasons for my dislike, though I think I could do so if pressed. For now I merely intend to differentiate fantasy from science fiction, a task that involves little more than remarking that while science fiction, as I have been arguing, maintains a respect for fact or presumptive fact, fantasy makes a point of flouting these; for a furniture of robots, space-ships, techniques, and equations it substitutes elves, broomsticks, occult powers, and incantations. It may be to the purpose to quote an utterance by Fredric Brown, one of the most ingenious and inventive, though not one of the most self-questioning, writers of science fiction. In the introduction to his volume of short stories, *Star Shine*, we find Brown, who also writes fantasy on occasion, attempting to distinguish the two modes. After referring to the Midas myth—"remember it?" he asks, an apposite question when we try to imagine his readership, and goes on to give a summary—Brown says:

> Let's translate that into science fiction. Mr. Midas, who runs a Greek restaurant in the Bronx, happens to save the life of an extraterrestrial from a far planet who is living in New York anonymously as an observer for the Galactic Federation, to which Earth for obvious reasons is not yet ready to be admitted.... The extraterrestrial, who is a master of sciences far beyond ours, makes a machine which alters the molecular vibrations of Mr. Midas's body so his touch will have a transmuting effect upon other objects. And so on. It's a science fiction story, or could be made to be one.

It might be thought that, to push it to the limit, a fantasy story could be turned into a science-fiction story merely by inserting a few lines of pseudo-scientific patter, and I would accept this as an extreme theoretical case, although I cannot think of an actual one. Even so, a difference which makes the difference between abandoning verisimilitude and trying to preserve it seems to me to make all the difference, and in practice the arbitrary and whimsical development of nearly every story of fantasy soon puts it beyond recovery by any talk of galactic federations or molecular vibrations. One parenthetical note: it should not be thought that no story dealing with elves and such can be science fiction. There are pixies and four-leafed clovers and cromlechs and the land of heart's desire in Eric Frank Russell's story "Rainbow's End," but these are mere apparatus in a sinister hypnotic attack on a band of interstellar explorers. Similarly, although vampirism is one of the staples of nineteenth-century fantasy, Richard Matheson's novel *I Am Legend* makes brilliantly ingenious and incidentally horrifying use of the myth for science-fiction purposes, whereby every traditional detail is explained along rational lines: the wooden stake through the heart, for instance, which put paid to Dracula and so many of his playmates, is necessary in order to maintain the distension of the wound—bullets and knives are no good for that job, and the microbe which causes vampirism is aerophobic.

While perhaps seeming to have kept our definition only distantly in view, I have in fact been rather deftly filling out and limiting its various implications. All that remains in this section is to describe a couple of codicils, kinds of narrative to be included on the grounds that they appeal to the same set of interests as science fiction in the sense defined, or at least are written and read by the same writers and readers. The first of these, numerically unimportant and readily disposed of, consists of stories about prehistoric man. Their existence can perhaps be blamed, for blame seems called for, on the fact that Wells wrote something called "A Story of the Stone Age"; I also note, though without at the moment doing more than note, that the subject reappears in *The Inheritors*, the second novel of the contemporary British writer William Golding, who comes nearer than anybody so far to being a serious author working within science fiction. But more of him later. The second supplementary category includes stories based on some change or disturbance or local anomaly in physical conditions. This accommodates several very familiar types of story, mostly involving novelties that threaten mankind. These may originate outside the Earth, as in Conan Doyle's "The Poison Belt" and Fred Hoyle's recent *The Black Cloud*, or on the Earth itself, as in John Christopher's *The Death of Grass*, published in the United States as *No Blade of Grass*. Alternatively, the author will chronicle some monstrous emergence arising from existing science and technology, especially, of course, the hydrogen bomb. The film industry has fallen gleefully upon that one, serving up a succession of beasts produced by mutation via radiation— giant ants, for instance, in *Them*—or else liberated from some primeval underground cavity by test explosions—*Rodan*, a Japanese film, made great play with a brace of giant armour-plated radioactive supersonic pterodactyls finally despatched by guided missiles. Menaces of this kind naturally antedate the hydrogen bomb: an early and, I should guess, very influential example is Wells's unpleasantly vivid "The Empire of the Ants," in which the anomaly in question consists of an increase in intelligence, not in mere bulk. Although this is treated as having arisen in the course of evolution, not under artificial stimulus, the story has an obvious place in the development of its category. Finally, I should point out here, or hereabouts, that the last ten years have seen a perceptible decline in the role played in science fiction by actual science. The space-ship, for example, for a long time remained novel enough to be worth some description: nowadays it is often no more than a means of introducing characters into an alien environment, referred to as casually as an aeroplane or a taxi. Many stories of the future, again, and these commonly of the more interesting kind, take as their theme changes in the political or economic realm, with science and technology reduced to background detail: the hero will be served with Venusian flying-monkey steaks by a robot waiter, but the main business of his evening will be to persuade his fellow-members of the General Motors clan to take up the sword against the Chrysler clan. "*Science* fiction" is every day losing some of its appropriateness as a name for science fiction, and the kind of rearguard action that is being fought on its behalf by the commentators, on the plea that politics and economics and psychology and anthropology and even ethics are really or nearly as much sciences as atomic physics, is chiefly valuable as an indication of a state of mind. In any event, no alternative nomenclature so far suggested is applicable enough to justify the huge task of getting it accepted in place of a term so firmly established as the present one.

To restate matters, then: science fiction presents with verisimilitude the human effects of spectacular changes in our environment, changes either deliberately willed or involuntarily suffered. I turn now to a brief and selective account of the ancestry of the form. To do so is at any rate to follow an apparently unbreakable habit, except perhaps as regards brevity, of those who discuss science fiction from within the field. To be perpetually recounting its own history marks the attainment of a kind of puberty in the growth of a mode or a style, and here we have yet another parallel in development between science fiction and jazz. The year 1441 is, I think, the earliest date to which anybody has yet traced back the origins of jazz; historians of science fiction are likely to start off with Plato and the Atlantis bits in the *Timaeus* and the *Critias*. From there they will wander forward, usually lending their account increased bulk and impressiveness by subsuming fantasy as well as science fiction under the irritating heading of "imaginative fiction," and taking in on the way the *Dialogues* of Pope Gregory I, the *Niebelungenlied* and *Beowulf*, the Arthurian romances, Thomas More, Gulliver, *The Mysteries of Udolpho, Frankenstein*, a lot about Poe, *Dracula*, Verne and Wells, arriving finally at the really climactic event, the foundation of *Amazing Stories* in 1926. (All these names, and very many more, are conscientiously discussed in L. Sprague de Camp's representative *Science Fiction Handbook*, published in 1953.) These manoeuvres, which leave the jazz historian doing the best he can with Ravel and Milhaud and what an honour it was for everybody when Stravinsky wrote the *Ebony Concerto* for Woody Herman's band, perhaps recall the attempts of the Renaissance apologists to establish the respectability of poetry as something neither obscene nor trivial, and there may be more than a merely verbal resemblance between the boastfulness of much science-fiction propaganda and Scaliger's assertion that

> Poetry represents things that are not, as if they were, and as they ought to be or might be. The poet makes another nature, hence he turns himself into another god: he also will create worlds.

Histories of science fiction, as opposed to "imaginative literature," usually begin, not with Plato or *The Birds* of Aristophanes or the *Odyssey*, but with a work of the late Greek prose romancer Lucian of Samosata. The distinction of this, the so-called *True History*, is that it includes the first account of an interplanetary voyage that the researchers have managed to unearth, but it is hardly science fiction, since it deliberately piles extravagance upon extravagance for comic effect:

> Relinquishing the pursuit, we set up two trophies, one for the infantry engagement on the spiders' webs, and one on the clouds for the air-battle. It was while we were thus engaged that our scouts announced the approach of the Cloud-centaurs, whom Phaethon had expected in time for the battle. They were indeed close upon us, and a strange sight, being compounded of winged horses and men; the human part, from the middle upwards, was as tall as the Colossus of Rhodes, and the equine the size of a large merchantman. Their number I cannot bring myself to write down, for fear of exciting incredulity.

It is no more than appropriate that Lucian's trip to the moon should be preceded by an encounter with some women who are grape-vines from the waist down and followed by sea-battles inside a whale's mouth, nor in particular that it should be accomplished by the travellers' ship being snatched up in a waterspout. Leaving aside the question whether there was enough science around in the second century to make science fiction feasible, I will merely remark that the sprightliness and sophistication of the *True History* make it read like a joke at the expense of nearly all early-modern science fiction, that written between, say, 1910 and 1940. I note finally Lucian's discovery that the men in the moon are of fantastic appearance and habits, but certainly not menacing in any way. The notion of nasty aliens is a comparatively recent one, although it is dominant in the early-modern period I have just defined. The contemporary alien tends to be not only not menacing, but so much better than man—morally rather than technologically—as to put him to shame. I am not quite sure what kind of deduction to draw from that graph, but there must be some.

It is not for a millennium and a half that, according to the canon, further attempts at a moon voyage appear. There might be thought to have been a good deal of science around in the 1630's, what with Kepler's work just finished, Galileo still doing his stuff, and astronomical observation improved to the point where for the first time the planet Mercury was observed in transit across the sun. However, Kepler's *Somnium*—published in 1634, the same year as the first English translation of Lucian's *True History*—evidently describes a trip to the moon in which demons are used as the power source, or rather the hero dreams that this is what is taking place. I find all this of compelling interest, but the plea of the science-fiction historians, that at that time you had little hope of getting to the moon except by dreaming about demons, fails to convince me that the *Somnium*, like the *True History*, is anything but fantasy. The same applies to Bishop Godwin's pro-Copernican romance, *Man in the Moone, or a Discourse of a Voyage Thither by Domingo Gonsales*, which was published in 1638, though probably written a good deal earlier, and was reprinted half a dozen times before the end of the century. Gonsales gets to the moon on a raft drawn by wild swans, a device which John Wilkins, chairman of the body which later became the Royal Society, considered to be quite sound in theory. The only point of much concern to us, however, is that the inhabitants of the moon are found to be what they regularly are in the earlier examples, creatures of a superior morality, any who fall far short of the required standard being infallibly detected and deported to Earth: "the ordinary vent for them," Godwin explains, "is a certain high hill in the North of America, whose people I can easily believe to be wholly descended of them."

I have given enough, I think, of the traditional roll call to establish its tendency, a heavy reliance on accidental similarities. This judgment certainly applies to the next book on everyone's list, Cyrano de Bergerac's *Voyage dans la Lune* (1650). After an abortive experiment with bottles of dew—the sun sucks up dew, you see—Cyrano gets to the moon in a chariot powered by rockets. It is much worse than pointless to take this as an "anticipation" of the engine recently fired at the moon by the Russians or of anything in recent literature, and the same is true of the fact that in Voltaire's *Micromégas* we have the first visit to Earth by an alien. One awaits the revelation that Spenser's Talus is the first, or at any rate an early, robot in English literature. A work more oddly omitted from science-fiction annals is *The Tempest*, in which the very features which must have caused it to be passed over—the comparatively factual outline, the approach by ship, instead of in a waterspout or by demon-propulsion—are the ones which should have brought it to notice. Furthermore, whatever *The Tempest* may be currently agreed to be about, I cannot help thinking that one of the things it is about is specialised knowledge, and whatever may be the relation currently devised between Jacobean science and magic, it would be safe to say that contemporary attitudes towards what we now see as two things were partly inseparable. Even if one resists the temptation to designate Caliban as an early mutant—"a freckled whelp," you remember, "not gifted with a human shape," but human in most other ways—and Ariel as an anthropomorphised mobile scanner, Prospero's attitude to them, and indeed his entire role as an adept, seems to some degree experimental as well as simply thaumaturgical. These considerations, I suggest, while not making the play anything but a very dilute and indirect influence on science fiction, do make it a distant anticipation. On a cruder level, the eccentric scientist-recluse and his beautiful daughter are an almost woefully familiar pair of stereotypes in all but the most recent science fiction, and, incidentally, large areas of what I might call the *Tempest* myth reappear in one of the best of the science-fiction films. The title was *Forbidden Planet*, which induces the reflection that planets have only in the last hundred years or less become the natural setting for this kind of writing; if we want to find early forms of it in days when the Earth was still incompletely explored and space was utterly inaccessible, the obvious place to look is not on other planets but in remote regions of our own, in particular, of course, undiscovered islands.

To mention *Gulliver's Travels* next is not likely to cause any surprise, nor, I hope, alarm. This work is clearly an ancestor of science fiction, and not on the grounds that Laputa is an early powered satellite, either. The claim rests firstly on the notorious pains taken by Swift to counterfeit verisimilitude in the details of his story. Without attempting to draw an exact parallel, I submit that this is rather like the methods of science fiction, at any rate in that it serves to dispel that air of arbitrariness, of having no further aim than to be striking, which is characteristic of most fantasy: the surprising behaviour of Lilliputian candidates for preferment would lose its effect, I take it, in an anti-realistic context. All that businesslike thoroughness in description, with everything given its dimensions, reappears noticeably in the work of Jules Verne, where it constitutes the chief—often the only—method of keeping the reader's disbelief in some state of suspension. The other science-fiction thing about *Gulliver's Travels* is that it presents, clearly enough, a series of satirical utopias, these being chronicled with a great power of inventing details that are to be consistent with some basic assumption. This point, where invention and social criticism meet, is the point of departure for a great deal of contemporary science fiction, and no work is more relevant than *Gulliver's Travels* to this part of our investigation.

Some of these remarks apply to two other island utopias: More's work and Bacon's *New Atlantis*. Of these, the Bacon fragment more strongly recalls science fiction, in that some of its marvels are technological, with research in meteorology, medicine, horticulture, and methods of conjuring, plus aeroplanes, submarines, and microtonal music using echo-chambers. But neither *Utopia* nor *The New Atlantis* match the intent and satirical preoccupation with the social surface that we find both in the Swift and in, for instance, Pohl and Kornbluth's *The Space Merchants*, from which I quoted earlier. Both More and Bacon are, of course, darlings of the science-fiction academics, together with many another writer who falls short of grim documentary realism. Typical omissions of more or less unexpectedness include Chaucer, whose "Squire's Tale" surely includes an account of an early flying machine, and the *Mundus Alter et Idem* attributed to Bishop Hall (1607). The *Mundus*, traditionally taken as a source of *Gulliver's Travels*, is a string of comic-satiric utopias—the gluttons' paradise where staircases are banned as difficult for eaters and dangerous for drinkers, the feminist paradise where men do all the chores and parliament is in perpetual session with everyone talking at once—that anticipates with weird precision another Pohl and Kornbluth novel, *Search the Sky*. The Gothic novel and its successors do get into the canon, but, with one large exception, these, while all-important in the ancestry of modern fantasy, scarcely prefigure science fiction. The exception can hardly help being *Frankenstein*, which, albeit in a distorted form, has had a posthumous career of unparalleled vigour; even old Dracula has less often been exhumed in cinematic form and has never been mated or allowed to re-galvanise himself. (I had better explain at this point that the contemporary trade-term applying to the monster is "android," a synthetic being roughly resembling a man, as opposed to a robot, which is a mere peripatetic machine.) The notable thing about Frankenstein the character is that, far from being possessed of supernatural powers, he is a physiologist with academic training, a feature he has retained in his modern incarnations, while altogether losing the sentimental Shelleyan quality that marked his original appearance. Frankenstein, in the popular mind, when not confused with his monster, is easily the most outstanding representative of the generic mad scientist who plagued bad early-modern science fiction and has now been fined down* into the better-adjusted but still unsociable and eccentric scientist who, often with a Miranda-like daughter-secretary in

* The career of the mad scientist flourishes unchecked in the modern juvenile comic book. Those who see in this fact a conspiratorial attempt to undermine public confidence in scientists (which would be a praiseworthy attempt anyhow, I should have thought) may be reassured to find that these days the mad scientist tends to be deprived of his laboratory by other, saner scientists, rather than being overthrown by the two-fisted space rangers. His Einstein haircut should be taken as a tribute to the universality of that great figure.

attendance, continues to head an occasional research project and figure in the hero's thoughts as the Old Man. More important science-fiction themes than this, however, have radiated from the original book. It is true that, as L. Sprague de Camp observes, "all the shambling horde of modern robots and androids are descendants of Frankenstein's sadly malevolent monster," but beyond this lies the whole notion of the artificial creation which turns and rends its master. Čapek's *R.U.R.* (1920) was perhaps the first modern treatment of this notion, which still regularly reappears, a recent instance being Robert Sheckley's story "Watchbird." Here an airborne device, programmed to detect and forestall aggressive intentions, ends by prohibiting most kinds of human action. This idea generalises into innumerable fictionalised sermons on the dangers of overgrown technology which I shall be detailing later. Before leaving *Frankenstein*, it is worth observing that a third aspect of the scientific character descends from it, that of the morally irresponsible researcher indifferent to the damage he may cause or render possible, a kind of person consciously described by Wells in *The Island of Dr. Moreau*, where animals are vivisected in an attempt to humanise them, and to all appearance unconsciously in *The Food of the Gods*, where Herakleophorbia IV, the growth-inducing compound, is thrown on to the rubbish dump and swilled down the drains and generally scattered over the countryside in a fantastically light-hearted spirit. The irresponsible type of scientist is not altogether separable from a fourth type with a diverse ancestry, that to whom science is a route to personal power.

Some mention of Poe is sadly difficult to avoid in the present context: it has to be admitted that while he was much more important, perhaps to the point of being all-important, in the development of fantasy, he had in one sense a very direct influence on the development of science fiction. Before examining this, it may be just about worth while recalling that Poe seems to have invented the detective story, or so I remember being told at school. Without attempting to rival the complexity of my comparative analysis of jazz and science fiction, I should like to assert flatly that detective fiction and science fiction are akin. There is a closely similar exaltation of idea or plot over characterisation, and some modern science fiction, like most detective fiction, but unlike the thriller, invites the reader to solve a puzzle. It is no coincidence—how could

it be?—that from Poe through Conan Doyle to Fredric Brown (the
Midas expert) the writer of the one will often have some sort of
concern with the other. Poe, at any rate, wrote a couple of stories
involving balloon flight, at that time still a novelty, and another
taking the destruction of the Earth as its point of departure. His
unfinished novel, however, *The Narrative of A. Gordon Pym*, though
sometimes cited, is a romance that wanders off into fantasy rather
than having anything to do with science fiction. Such interest as it
holds for us lies in the fact that Jules Verne's *An Antarctic Mystery* is a
continuation, albeit an incoherent one, of the *Pym* narrative, and it
is clear from innumerable resemblances, as well as from his own
admission, that Verne learnt more from Poe than from any other
writer.

With Verne we reach the first great progenitor of modern science
fiction. In its literary aspect his work is, of course, of poor quality, a
feature certainly reproduced with great fidelity by most of his
successors. Although interspersed on occasion with fast and exciting
narrative, for instance in the episode where Captain Nemo and his
associates find their twenty-thousand-league voyage interrupted by
the Antarctic ice pack, the story line is cluttered up again and again
by long explanatory lectures and bald undramatised flashbacks.
Even the more active passages are full of comically bad writing:

> What a scene! The unhappy man, seized by the tentacle and
> fastened to its blowholes, was balanced in the air according to the
> caprice of this enormous trunk. He was choking, and cried out, *"A
> moi! à moi!"* (Help! help!). Those French words caused me a
> profound stupor. Then I had a countryman aboard, perhaps several!
> I shall hear that heartrending cry all my life!
>
> The unfortunate man was lost. Who would rescue him from that
> powerful grasp? Captain Nemo threw himself on the poulp, and with
> his hatchet cut off another arm. His first officer was fighting with
> rage against other monsters that were climbing the sides of the
> *Nautilus.* The crew were fighting with hatchets.
>
> The Canadian, Conseil, and I dug our arms into the fleshy masses.
> A violent smell of musk pervaded the atmosphere. It was horrible.

One would have to blame Verne's translator for some of those
ineptitudes, but such was the form in which the novels reached
English-speaking readers, none of whom, to my knowledge, has
bothered to complain. The story and the ideas were the thing.

These ideas, the scientific ones at least, have naturally got a bit dated: the helicopter with seventy-four horizontal screws, the tunnel to the centre of the Earth, the moon-ship shot out of a gun at a speed that would have pulped the travellers before they were clear of the barrel. But these errors hardly matter, any more than Swift's Brobdingnagians cease to be impressive when we reason that they would have broken most of their bones whenever they tried to stand up. It matters hardly more that Verne did successfully foretell the guided missile, nor that this extract from *Five Weeks in a Balloon* (1862) has a bearing on events of eighty years later:

> "Besides," said Kennedy, "the time when industry gets a grip on everything and uses it to its own advantage may not be particularly amusing. If men go on inventing machinery they'll end by being swallowed up by their own inventions. I've often thought that the last day will be brought about by some colossal boiler heated to three thousand atmospheres blowing up the world."
>
> "And I bet the Yankees will have a hand in it," said Joe.

The general prophecy about invention overreaching itself is clearly far more interesting than the particular glimpse of something like the nuclear bomb, or rather of its possible outcome. Verne's importance is that, while usually wrong or implausible or simply boring in detail, his themes foreshadow a great deal of contemporary thinking, both inside and outside science fiction.

As regards the mode itself, Verne developed the tradition of the technological utopia, presenting in *The Begum's Fortune* a rival pair of these, the one enlightened and paternalistic, the other totalitarian and warlike. This was published in 1879, so it is no surprise to find that the nice utopia is French and the nasty one German. There are also several novels virtually initiating what has become a basic category of science fiction, the satire that is also a warning, and it is here that Verne is of some general interest. Thus in *Round the Moon*, after the projectile has fallen back into the sea—at a speed of 115,200 miles an hour, incidentally, and without hurting anyone inside—we find a company being founded to "develop" the moon after a fashion that anticipates *The Space Merchants*. The sequel to *Round the Moon, The Purchase of the North Pole*, involves not only the said purchase on the part of the Baltimore Gun Club, the people who set up the cannon to fire the moon-projectile, but a scheme whereby a monstrous explosion shall alter the inclination of the Earth's axis and so bring the polar region into the temperate zone. Since parts of the civilised world would correspondingly be shifted into new polar regions, the response of officialdom is unfavourable. However, the explosion takes place, and only an error in the calculations preserves the *status quo*. The notion of an advancing technology increasing the destructive power of unscrupulousness reappears on a smaller scale in *The Floating Island*, where the huge artifact breaks up in mid-ocean as a result of rivalry between two financial cliques. The book closes with a straightforward Vernean sermon on the dangers of scientific progress considered as an embodiment of human arrogance. The heavy moral tone of this and many passages in the other books is among the less fortunate of Verne's legacies to modern science fiction, and some of his other anticipations, if they are properly that, give no cause for congratulation. In particular, his sexual interest is very thin: Phileas Fogg, the hero of *Around the World in Eighty Days*, does pick up an Indian princess in the course of his travels, but we discover almost nothing about her, and Fogg treats her with an inflexible courtesy which goes beyond mere Victorianism and which any girl of spirit might find subtly unflattering. Even the villains rarely do so much as aspire to lechery. It is in his political tone, which, however vague and eccentric, is nearly always progressive, and even more in his attitude to technology, fascinated but sceptical and at times tinged with pessimism, that Verne's heritage is most interesting and valuable: his last book, *The Eternal Adam*, is a kind of proleptic elegy for the collapse of Western civilisation. These are the considerations which go some way to override his ineptitude and pomposity, his nineteenth-century boys'-story stuffiness, and make him, not only in a science-fiction sense, recognisably modern.

Whatever else he may or may not have been, Jules Verne is certainly to be regarded as one of the two creators* of modern

---

* There were, of course, innumerable other ancestors of secondary importance. The volume of utopian literature in the second half of the nineteenth century is huge, and its range stretches all the way from tract-like, plotless dogmatisms of politics, economics, or religion to adventure stories with a few ideas in them. Some of these works were of great and prolonged popularity: the classic instance is Edward Bellamy's *Looking Backward*, with its world-wide sale and its dozens of rejoinders. The vogue of this kind of writing was such that Gilbert and Sullivan,

science fiction; the other, inevitably enough, is H. G. Wells. To treat Wells as such, rather than as the first important practitioner in an existing mode, is no denigration. Rather, it takes account of the fact that all his best and most influential stories appeared between 1895 and 1907, before science fiction had separated itself from the main stream of literature, and so were written, published, reviewed, and read as "romances" or even adventure stories. The expected comparison with Verne, made often enough at the time (though repudiated by both), now shows not only a huge disparity in literary merit but certain differences in the direction of interest. A main preoccupation of Verne's, as I said, was technology itself, "actual possibilities," as Wells put it, "of invention and discovery," and this holds true equally when what were possibilities to Verne are impossibilities or grotesque improbabilities to us. The long scientific lectures interpolated in his stories—"If I created a temperature of 18°, the hydrogen in the balloon will increase by 18/480s, or 1,614 cubic feet" and so on—these lectures, however tedious, are highly germane to what Verne was doing. Wells, on the other hand, is nearly always concerned only to fire off a few phrases of pseudo-scientific patter and bundle his characters away to the moon or the 803rd century with despatch. Verne himself saw this point all right, and complained after reading (rather cursorily, it seems) *The First Men in the Moon*:

> I make use of physics. He fabricates. I go to the moon in a cannon-ball discharged from a gun. There is no fabrication here. He goes to Mars [*sic*] in an airship [*sic*], which he constructs of a metal that does away with the law of gravitation. That's all very fine, but show me this metal. Let him produce it.

It is often said that Wells's main interest was not in scientific advance as such but in its effect on human life. Although this is true of some of his works, as we shall see in a moment, it is patently not true of the ones which had the most immediate effect on the growth of science fiction. Indeed, in this respect the Verne of *The Floating*

---

who had a sharp eye for fashions in taste if for nothing else, thought it worth a whole operetta, *Utopia Ltd.* (first performed in 1893), which I have so far been unable to see performed. Nor was this an interest confined to specialists or cranks, as is testified by the existence of utopian works by Bulwer Lytton, Samuel Butler, W. H. Hudson, William Morris, and William Dean Howells.

Island or *The Purchase of the North Pole* seems distinctly more contemporary than the Wells of *The Time Machine* or *The Invisible Man*. The real importance of these stories is that they liberated the medium from dependence on extrapolation and in so doing initiated some of its basic categories. The time machine itself, the Martians and their strange irresistible weapons in *The War of the Worlds*, the monsters in the first half of *The Food of the Gods*, the other world coterminous with ours in "The Plattner Story," the carnivorous plant in "The Flowering of the Strange Orchid," all these have had an innumerable progeny. What is noticeable about them is that they are used to arouse wonder, terror, and excitement, rather than for any allegorical or satirical end. When the Time Traveller finds that mankind will have become separated into two races, the gentle ineffectual Eloi and the savage Morlocks, the idea that these are descended respectively from our own leisured classes and manual workers comes as a mere explanation, a solution to the puzzle; it is not transformed, as it inevitably would be in a modern writer, into a warning about some current trend in society. *The Invisible Man* is only very incidentally concerned with the notion that a scientific discovery may be dangerously two-edged; the novel is about the problems, firstly of being, secondly of catching, an invisible man. "The Country of the Blind," which is science fiction of the physical-change variety, is about what it would be like for a sighted person in a country of the blind: the proverb about the one-eyed man being king there doubtless inspired the story, but its theme is a concretisation, not a daring imaginative statement, of the untruthful aspect of that proverb. A contemporary writer, again, would have used the proposed blinding of the hero as a climactic point for the enfilading of our intolerance towards exceptional talents; Wells throws this away in an aside, giving us the hero of an adventure story in danger, not the representative of anything being threatened with anything representative. Dr. Moreau's beast-men are beast-men, not symbolic puppets enacting a view of beasts and men, or of men. *The First Men in the Moon* admittedly has some satirical discussions of war and human irrationality, together with one of several early anticipations of the conditioning-during-sleep idea Huxley developed in *Brave New World*, but Wells's main drive here is simple delight in invention, in working out an alien ecology, typical of what I might call primitive science fiction.

Despite the fluent imaginativeness of the stories mentioned, the most forceful of Wells's romances is the strongly Verne-like *The War in the Air* of 1907. This curious synthesis of World Wars I, II, and III, with Germany attacking the United States before both are overwhelmed by a Chinese-Japanese coalition, is certainly concerned with the effect of technology on mankind, since the one is made to reduce the other to barbarism, and being both satire and warning, it has, in the science-fiction context at any rate, an unmistakably modern ring. *The War in the Air*, however, rates comparatively little attention from the commentators, as do Wells's utopian romances and their not-so-remote ancestor of the early Fabian period, William Morris's *News From Nowhere. Men Like Gods*, with its nudism, or *In the Days of the Comet*, where a strange gas so fills humanity with loving-kindness that everyone gets started on companionate marriage, have none of the fire of the early Wells, and give a soporific whiff of left-wing crankiness, but their virtual exclusion from the modern science-fiction canon is surprising. This part of Wells's output anticipated, but evidently did not influence, later developments. Even "A Story of the Days to Come," an early and lively piece, never gets a mention, and yet it forecasts the modern satirical utopia with fantastic exactness: advertising matter is everywhere bawled out of loudspeakers, phonographs have replaced books, mankind is urbanized to the point where agriculturalists commute in reverse, huge trusts reign supreme, an army of unemployables is maintained by a kind of international poorhouse called the Labour Company, all children are brought up in State crèches, deviates get their antisocial traits removed by hypnosis, dreams can be obtained to order, and as a last detail, a prophecy so universal nowadays as to justify panic in razor-blade circles, men don't shave any more, they use depilatories. Quite likely Wells will soon get all, instead of part, of the recognition as pioneer he clearly deserves.

Science Fiction and Literature

by Robert Conquest

A type of writing whose friends among post-war practitioners of ordinary fiction include such names as William Golding, Kingsley Amis and Angus Wilson, scarcely needs defending in any ordinary sense. On the other hand, science fiction is a type of imaginative writing which has not been much dealt with in the vast literature about literature which is such a mark, or possibly stigma, of our epoch; and it is doubtless true that anyone prepared to look at it is unlikely to take the conventional critical trappings very seriously. But in any case, it is a large field, in which standards vary considerably, and in this sort of essay one is almost obliged to be sketchy and selective, and make a few general points, rather than "rigorously" assess.

A good amount of perspicuous comment on the nature and virtues of science fiction has appeared—in Mr. Edmund Crispin's introductions to his yearly anthologies, for instance. I want to deal mainly with something different—the illumination it casts on the nature of our literary habits and on our culture generally. It is specially suitable to do this now, when things have settled down and a first premature burst of modishness is fortunately over. This brief band-wagon period, during which dons reviewed science fiction with an enthusiasm tempered by patronage and stultified by ignorance, did no good to anyone, and can hardly be said to have had much effect on the Literary Mind.

The habits, one might almost say the reflexes, of a culture's attitude to its literature depend on the workings of the minds of people like critics and general kulturträger rather than on writers themselves. The generalized cultured man is interested in ballet and in music, and in literature *as such* rather than anything which it

"Science Fiction and Literature" by Robert Conquest. From *The Critical Quarterly*, V (1963), 355–67. Reprinted by permission of Robert Conquest.

might be thought of as dealing with. Creative writers are often very different—tone-deaf, like Yeats, or brazenly philistine, like Mark Twain, or concerned with the message more than the writing, like Tolstoy. And they are interested in the actualities and potentialities of the phenomenal world for their own sakes, not merely as background for the subjective (compare Auden with his lesser contemporaries).

We are all inclined to take our particular form of culture for granted; our literature too. Yet Western literature, as it has been in the last two hundred years or so, is a very special and eccentric sort of thing compared with any other. What distinguishes it is the extraordinary, dominating position of the novel of character.

Literary taste has therefore involved acceptance of the conventions implicit in this. Moreover, under present conditions the average cultivated man is likely to be considerably more introverted than the average. And thus he is likely to have a special bias in favour of the literature of "character" and to see in it a significance and superiority which is entirely a matter of his personal taste. (The main works which are not novels of character and are yet lapped up by this over-introverted audience are those which, like Kafka's, are centred on *angst*—a highly revealing exception.) The claims usually made for the psychological novel are that it is more human and more realistic than any other. But it was a novelist who complained of "ascribing to others the feelings you would feel if you were in their place. It is this (among much else) that makes novels so false." Even Tolstoy's private life may make us feel that he was not very understanding about real human beings. Fiction is fiction, moreover; and the production of the suspension of disbelief, which I take to be the crux of the novelist's art, can yet only be called "realism" as a sort of conventional label.

To anyone interested at all in literature science fiction should be a most curious and significant phenomenon, for two reasons. In the first place, it is a tradition which has sprung up almost entirely outside the general flow of literature. And in the second place it makes a fairly clean break with principles which have come to be rather taken for granted in a novel since the Eighteenth Century, rather as the unities used to be in French drama. Of course, to take literary conventions for granted, and when they are broken to retort hotly that anything outside them is "not literature" is a piece of unthinking automatism. Science fiction here performs the service of making people think—or at worst making them show that they are incapable of thinking. In either case it is a good thing to know where we stand.

There have always been two sorts of imagination in literature. One has been fascinated by the variations of human feelings and actions within contexts which are taken for granted. The other is inclined to take the human behaviour largely for granted and to be interested more in environmental changes—expressed, certainly, in the effect on human behaviour. The difference is, if you like, that between the *Comédie Humaine* and the *Divina Commedia*. There is now this inclination to hold that the *psychological* interest is somehow higher and more important than the other. It is in childhood that the faculty of intellectual, objective curiosity develops, while it is only in adolescence that introspection begins. Both are necessary human qualities. Both carry equal charges of imagination—even of awe. There has been, in the last century or so, a tendency in the literary world greatly to exaggerate the importance of the adolescent component, though this has not been so noticeable among the creators. Literary intellectuals are inclined to look down on the scientist, the imaginative man whose faculty is largely concentrated on the objective side, as childish. Yet the order in which the components are assembled is quite irrelevant to their importance in the completed adult being. It is reasonable for a balance to exist, and for various reasons the tendency has been for one side of the thing to be grossly hypertrophied. To some extent this is a self-perpetuating process. Introspective literature attracts introspective critics who create introspective canons and anathematise what does not appeal to them. And it is a good sign for literature in general that things have altered a little.

For over the last few years there has been some change in the attitude to science fiction. For a long time it was regarded as an outré form of "mass-culture." It was associated with the sensationalism of its lowest type (as absurd an attitude, really, as to condemn novels about love—e.g. *Anna Karenina*—on account of the sentimental women's serial). Now, however, it seems to be coming back into the main stream of literature, from which it only diverged a few hundred years ago. For quite a time there have been at least some literary men who have read science fiction without any special condescension.

Even so, very few "intellectual" readers have come to it except in an accidental fashion, leading to curious misapprehensions. To have read (as is common) only the work of John Wyndham and Ray Bradbury is rather as if one's knowledge of the European novel were confined to Trollope and Firbank. Mr. Wyndham is, of course, the Trollope. He is an old and experienced science-fiction writer, of whom it would not be unfair to say that his work appeared for decades, and rightly, in ephemeral pulp magazines. Then he suddenly produced *The Day of the Triffids.* This small masterpiece attains its effect by superimposing extraordinary events on a slow-moving, ordinary, very English background of persons and feelings. This is an old way of doing it and is certainly an admirable and legitimate one. If I use a word like parochial about it, that is not in the least to denigrate it. Just the same, it does not get you far in a field where the norm is by no means the society of here and now with the extraordinary just superimposed on it, though one can see and welcome the reasons for its wide acceptance by a larger public.

Mr. Bradbury's success is of a quite different sort. He too started off as a pulp writer. But his later success is a peculiar one. He is not highly regarded in science fiction circles proper, apart from the occasional story. His "Golden Apples of the Sun" appeared in the *Observer* with great ceremony. It was a reprint from the third-rate *Planet Stories.* Why, then, has he received such praise? The answer is probably to be sought under several heads: first, he goes in for "fine writing"; secondly his mood is, in a very crude way, one of anti-scientific "humanism," if you can call it that. Then, he has that sort of Saroyan atmosphere of conscious naivety—moms and so on—which for some probably not very creditable reason often goes down big in the literary world. But a final motive might be something like this: he is a writer who literary-minded people can feel is science-fiction. They would perhaps be a little ignorant, if they did not read a little. They find Bradbury, but not science-fiction proper, tolerable. Thus he becomes the science-fiction writer of the person who doesn't really like science-fiction, much as Colin Wilson was briefly the philosopher of people who don't really like philosophy. This is just a trifle unfair to Bradbury, and it is worth recalling that all these faults of his become tolerable when he writes pure fantasy—ghost stories—in which a certain amount of manner goes very well. And, indeed, some of his "s.f." is scarcely to be thought of as such.

To say what is meant by science-fiction always leads to a definition which excludes at least something that any s.f. reader would ordinarily include. The genre tapers off gradually through all sorts of borderline stories—sometimes barely distinguishable from straight fiction on the one hand and sometimes hard to disentangle from pure fantasy on the other. All the same there are reasons for saying something about the coverage of the term.

The mere word science-fiction is inclined to irritate the too literary reader by raising indigestibly what he rightly or wrongly thinks of as science: the gadgetry and inventions of physicists. In practice science-fiction ranges over every type of story in which the centre of attention is on the results of a possible, though not actual, change in the conditions of life. This may merely involve describing what happens when a man is transferred to the moon. It may be a more or less social satire—the extrapolation of something in present society into an exaggerated future. It may be psychological—like a story of the future, "Beyond Bedlam," which once appeared in *Galaxy,* about a time when the psychological tensions destructive of society have been resolved by the withdrawal of clashing personality facets in every individual into two distinct personalities, each of which has the use of the body for a week at a time: (it was well worked out and of course the greatest social crime consisted of extending your tenure by various tricks and committing adultery with your wife's alter ego). But the variations are wide, and lead to the reflection that "science-fiction" is in some ways an unfortunate name. "Possibility fiction" might have been better.

The centre of interest may well not be "hero" at all. But this does not mean that the character has to be a "cardboard" one. Just as in some of the ordinary novels of America, a few hints are sufficient to create an adult effect without distracting attention from the main issues. The sort of literary problems presented are quite new. For example, there is an excellent story by Robert Heinlein ("By His Bootstraps") whose hero is quite simply *Time* and the paradoxes involved in time travel. The main character is transferred to and fro between a very distant future and the same point of time nowadays. The result is that he appears in his own room *now* three times as far as his life-line is concerned but simultaneously from the time point of view, i.e. he lives through a scene three times at later and later points in his own life. The artistic difficulties of a story of this sort are apparent at once. It could so easily be completely wooden, certainly. But also it could fall over the other way and make the character so rich, if you like, that the main point of the story would be obscured.

Nor is it true that because character is not the focus, subtlety as well as intelligence is any less involved. Even at a very crude "material" level, this can be shown, as when, in the "Null-A" novels, van Vogt provides a philosophical basis both for instantaneous long distance travel, and for telepathy between carefully controlled near-identical twins, by the concept of similarity. Absolute identity implies identity as to spatial position also: so that the instrument ("distorter") which forces similarity to an enormously high degree, down to electronic level, by that act forces a spatial transfer of the one "similarised" object to the location of its model. One or two queries naturally arise in our minds, but the sophistication of the concept shows something of the subtlety of which science fiction is capable even in dealing with gross movement. This illustrates the fact that the muscles of the imagination need more than one sort of exercise. The literary mind is often defective in imaginative capacity of a type it has not been trained for or simply does not have the potentialities for.

There are many ways in which science fiction illuminates matters of literature and of culture far beyond its own sphere. For example, it shows the comparatively primitive and irrational basis on which all our tastes in reading arise in the first place. Kingsley Amis, in his *New Maps of Hell*, describes how, coming across a pile of early American s.f. pulps in Woolworth's before the war, he at once knew that this was his kind of thing. John Christopher, the science fiction author, has described his initiation in exactly the same way. (The same happened to the present writer, though he had, as one imagines Amis and Christopher had, been reading Wells and Verne since the age of about eight.) The point is that we have here, as doubtless with thousands of others, a case of immediate, temperamental taste, in which there can be little question of training, education or even "culture" in the ordinary sense. It was not, of course, an exclusive taste. Many of us who have read modern science-fiction ever since those magazines of our early 'teens, have also become involved in ordinary ("mainstream," as science-fiction writers call it) literature in various ways, even to the extent of writing it. But it indicates, what is perhaps too often forgotten in sophisticated analysis, the essentially primitive, basic nature of our views and tastes in literature. I would imagine that with most people, in other spheres too, the essential is much the same: one or more theophanies in their early 'teens—Swinburne's poetry, perhaps, or Pound's—which all their later development is either elaboration of or reaction from, or both.

Science-fiction has its history and its roots, and it is common for books and essays on the subject to produce a most respectable pedigree going back to Lucian of Samosata (or even, if it comes to that, to the Timaeus) and tracing the development from those times through people like Bishop Wilkins, who wrote an account of a lunar voyage in the early seventeenth century, Cyrano de Bergerac, and so on. But all that seems rather beside the point. It is doubtful that these people had an influence on each other, let alone on science-fiction as it has developed in the last half-century. The first true primitive classics are, naturally, Jules Verne and H. G. Wells. Purely technically, in regard to the literary spirit of their writings, it is not too difficult to derive these authors. Verne has been held up by some French critics as a sort of mile-post of romanticism—something like Delacroix in painting. But it is rather pointless to speak of science-fiction as such as involving a particular mood or movement, if only because as we all know there has been plenty of s.f. with very different attitudes. The real question is, how or why did the science-fiction writers adopt their particular *themes*. Or rather, not simply the themes, but a whole method of regarding the suitability of special matter. It is not a *literary* derivation that Verne and Wells show us on this point. The new components of their work were injected sideways, as it were, into the literary stream from outside, from the huge arena in which creative Homo Faber had erected a whole new attitude—of science and (at that time) of optimism.

Verne and Wells were not as isolated as they seem in retrospect. Quite a lot of similar though inferior work was being produced at the time. And it never really ceased. But Verne died fifty years ago.

And Wells was in many ways a very untypical figure. Science fiction as a genre on its own should really be considered as having been created much later and quite apart from Wells.

It is usual to trace it to an extremely poor story called "Ralph 124 C 41" by Hugo Gernsback, which came out during the First World War. It may seem a little incredible to shuffle Wells off like this (and, in addition people like Rudyard Kipling and E. M. Forster were occasionally writing what can reasonably be called science fiction). But it is not a rare thing for a new art form to start off at a very crude level—Latin rhymed poetry is an instance. Gernsback's writing is quite insignificant. It was just one of many stories being written in a rather ham-handed fashion by people whose imaginations were turned in the science-fiction direction, but whose literary gifts were pretty negative. Why it is taken to mark an epoch is continuity: Gernsback was a magazine editor who some years later founded the first permanent science fiction magazine, *Amazing Stories*. In the late twenties and early thirties this magazine and the two which followed it, *Wonder Stories* and (as it was then called) *Astounding Stories*, laid the basis for modern science fiction. The quality of the writing, as might be expected, was low. And, curiously enough, for a time it gradually got lower still.

The reason for this was that at the beginning there were two rather different ways in which the stories were bad. Some were written by German or German-American professors whose qualifications were usually given; and very impressive these often were. Their stories usually consisted of highly technical future developments, complete with footnotes explaining the details. The action was often simply of a naive young hero (if that is the word) being shown round some island or planetary Utopia whose social arrangements seemed to indicate that the professor held over-optimistic views about the regulation of the human passions.

The other type of writing gave the impression that it was being produced by people in their late 'teens, with highly developed imaginations about the shape and characteristics of extra-terrestrial monsters and a fair capability of describing hair's breadth escapes, but with rather stereotyped ideas about the motivations—even of the monsters. Though less adult, these were on the whole more popular than the professorial ones, and rightly so, and they crowded them out.

The significant thing is that most of these stories really were written by very young people. They had started writing in this unsophisticated way because they had, however crudely, something imaginative they wanted to say. And they grew up! By about 1939–40 a number of them had matured in every possible way. And, in many cases, they had learnt to write. If we take a man like Isaac Asimov and look at his earliest work it is quite a shock. I know that many people who became addicted to science fiction had the luck, as I did myself, to grow up with these magazines. For the boy of eleven or twelve the early crudities were perfectly all right. And as he grew out of them they grew out of them too. What had happened was a very rare and curious thing. A whole series of writers writing almost solely in magazines devoted to their single genre had developed *quite separately from ordinary literary origins.* No doubt this should be qualified by saying that the ordinary literary influences seeped across in a general way. But it is only a qualification.

A. E. van Vogt's story "Black Destroyer" (later incorporated in *The Voyage of the Space Beagle*) appeared in *Astounding* in August 1939, and it is often taken as the beginning of the golden age which got properly going about 1943 and began to taper off a little around 1948. (To my mind the Beagle stories were better before they were linked together by a central character, the nexialist Grosvenor.) Maturity brought variation. (But the vehicle for years was almost solely *Astounding*, under John Campbell's inspired editorship. True science fiction was for long never seen in hard covers. The odd exceptions were brought out by specialist presses in small editions— van Vogt's *Slan* for instance was printed in Pennsylvania in an edition of 2,000, whose price five years later was something like ten or twelve times above par.)

A point that often escapes literary critics dealing with the genre is just how very different and individual its best writers are. It might seem to somebody considering the whole business in an abstract way that all its writers would be rather alike. It was Anatole France, himself an enormous stylist, who pointed out that the best authors often do not write very well. Though there are fine stylists and workmanlike artificers among science fiction writers, it is true that some of the most effective have major faults of a more or less superficial nature. Van Vogt, to my mind one of the most extraordinary in the field, is an example. Not only is his work erratic in general, and sometimes constructed in an almost incomprehensible manner, but he often heavily overwrites, even in his best work.

If we divide science fiction into two main moods, one might be said to lay out its imaginary world coolly and calmly' and gain its effects by a cumulative objectivity; and the other which hustles the reader into acceptance by sheer high pace and obsessiveness.' Van Vogt is a great figure in this second school. In a different way Alfred Bester, whose work is well known over here, does something of the same sort in his *Tiger! Tiger!* and *The Demolished Man.* Similarly, a division might be made between stories of the extreme and fantastic future and work fairly rigorously covering changes which can be more or less definitely foreseen from present knowledge—going into the next fifty to a hundred years, perhaps, at the most. In this latter the most effective stuff is clear and simple—Arthur Clarke's *The Sands of Mars* or Robert Heinlein's *The Man Who Sold the Moon* and so on.

This raises a small but itself significant issue: what constitutes authenticity? For example, it is completely established that a human being could not survive on Mars breathing its atmosphere. A science-fiction writer must either give his human visitor to Mars an oxygen mask, or he must indicate that the atmosphere has in some way been changed. If you say "what does it matter?" you are putting yourself in the position of a man who sees nothing odd in reading an ordinary imaginative novel about the Irish countryside in which the villagers are, for some unexplained reason, Negroes. A similar problem sometimes arises in historical novels. Certainly it depends on the amount of knowledge a reader might reasonably be supposed to have. Professor Trevor Roper would be put out by anachronisms in a novel of Elizabethan life which the rest of us would scarcely notice. Still, there are limits, and I trust that we would all have an uneasy feeling if we read about Sir Walter Raleigh greeting the Queen by raising his bowler hat.

How much science, then, should we know? It really seems that nowadays there are quite a lot of literary people who regard themselves as educated in spite of what one might almost call a reckless and wilful ignorance of even the most ordinary bits of scientific information. After all, it is not as if anyone pretends that even a moderately educated man can rely entirely on artistic information. He would be expected to know a little elementary geography, say: that Australia has no land connection with Asia or that Mount Everest is not situated in the Alps. But there is a point at which compulsive ignorance sets in. To read some criticism of science-fiction, and indeed of science, one would imagine that it was a positive insult to suggest that knowledge about the surface of the Moon is available, let alone desirable. (Curiously enough, this does not prevent literary people, sometimes, from making pronouncements in scientific fields of which they know nothing. In one of the better Sunday papers a year or so ago there was a perfectly serious review by an excellent poet and critic of a book basing itself on the wholly crackpot Hoerbiger theory of cosmology.)

To a large number of such people science-fiction is more or less identified with a single theme: the interplanetary rocket. This is really rather a misapprehension. What is true is that a large proportion of science-fiction is set in the future, for obvious reasons. And our grandchildren, unless indeed they are barbarians living in a radioactive desert (a theme not ignored by science-fiction), will live in a world in which the most unavoidably obvious new development will be interplanetary travel. Thus a writer producing any story of a civilised Twenty-First Century is bound to provide some background of space-travel simply in the interests of authenticity. But to anyone who is used to it it is no more *intrusive* than the ships are, by which Swift was able to transfer Gulliver to unknown islands at a time when such existed.

As to the future, a good many things have become taken for granted and have even become traditional. As Mr. R. C. Churchill says, it may be surprising to learn that there are traditions about the future, but such is the case. In a science-fiction radio play of Mr. Amis's I noticed one of them: "blaster." In the old days the side-arm of the future explorer or duellist or whatever was given a variety of names, usually of a highly unlikely technical nature, as who should call a Colt revolver a "multiple lead projector." And their workings were frequently described. Nowadays it is seldom that this is bothered with, and we simply have the "blaster." There are other things of the same sort. The main settlement on the Moon is called Luna City by quite a number of authors. Travel faster than light, obviously necessary for certain plots, but impossible in

Einsteinian space, is carried on by "space warp" through "sub-space" or "hyper-space." One of the oddest of these bits of terminology is the currency of the future, which is almost always the "credit." And that, I think, is a convenient symbol of the absence of chauvinism in this largely American or Anglo-American art. Of course it is usually the Western culture which is projected, at least into the near future, for obvious reasons. But it is quite normal for Mr. Heinlein to give us a solar system ruled by a king of the Dutch royal house, or Mr. Sprague de Camp to have as the dominant language of the interstellar period Portuguese—the language of the leading nation, Brazil, and its organisation Viagens Interplanetarias.

The genre has always included sociological and other satire, and here we have a problem not confined to science-fiction. It is a truism that if a polemic in novel form is to be more than a rather boring tract the main interest must be in the story itself and not in its message. As Yeats says of one of his plays:

> "Players and painted stage took all my love
> And not those things that they were emblems of"

A story like Pohl and Kornbluth's *The Space Merchants* (originally called *Gravy Planet*) might be called a satire by *reductio ad absurdum* on that aspect of modern commercial civilisation in which heavy advertising strives, most anti-socially, to secure the maximum consumption of everything. But the story itself is the thing. Neither the constructive reality of the world they are describing nor the tempo of the development is broken up simply for "shrewd hits." Masterpieces like *The Sleeper Awakes* and *1984* need all their power to carry quite a small load of dead wood, and when it comes to Mr. Ray Bradbury's *Fahrenheit 451* the preaching is so crude that it is rather rare for anyone to like it except those who approve of it as a tract.

For whatever its satirical or other virtues, fiction is a dead loss if it does not present an imaginary world which is deeply believable, acceptable. Only thus, in some as yet unexplained way, are our own feelings given sustenance, our own imagination given exercise. Science-fiction is simply a neglected, and wrongly neglected, way of doing this. The particular type of excitement to be found in science-fiction is not, perhaps, entirely new: there is something of the same feeling in Elizabethan writing, when our culture's imagination was strongly directed to the possibilities of unknown lands, to Dr. Dee's projects for discovering the philosopher's stone, and so on, and when Utopias set in a quite imaginary Virginia entered into the creative literature. (It is not the mere piece of information that someone will bring us back in the next few decades about Martian vegetation—say—that is significant. It is the act of reducing the unknown to order that gives it its power and excitement.) Another side to this future-discoveries-and-explorations theme is even more traditional—simply that an active and educated literature has usually, or often, been written by the man who has kept his imagination at the frontiers of expanding knowledge.

Anthropologists have held that a great literature, a cultural expansion, often goes with a physical expansion—that the ages of Greek and Elizabethan exploration were not accidentally those of great literature. And that is only taking it at its crudest, the mere act of landing on Sicily or America—or Mars. In a culture like our own the frontiers of knowledge have all sorts of other directions, and if a writer is being truly what I would call modern, he is at least aware of them. As for subjects, naturally he is not compelled to take any special themes. And it goes without saying that it is no good trying to make poetry, for example, modern by filling it with rockets—like the tractors and travelling-cranes which infested the poorer verse of the Thirties. Yet, if one wishes for a physical object to write about, I cannot but feel that the rocket is preferable to the rood-screen.

A striking thing about the science fiction of the 1890's is where it goes wrong in its predictions about the 1950's. Technical details, of course, are not always right—usually the speed of technological advance has been greatly under-estimated. There are inclined to be airships and moving pavements. But even in the closest predictions the great failure is on the social side. People go on behaving much the same as in the nineties. The heavily-clothed women are tended with smelling salts as they have the vapours in spaceships. The ballistic missile is anticipated, but not the Bikini bathing dress—nor if it comes to that, changes in furniture and general taste. One would not necessarily expect the details of such changes to be got right, but in quasi-predictive science-fiction it seems reasonable to hypothesise *some* sort of changes and pretty radical ones. On the whole the modern writers avoid these traps—at least they make an effort to do so.

If you start reading and judging science-fiction more or less for the first time there is one thing to be warned against. Ingenuity is one of the great virtues of the genre. But it is on the whole extremely rare nowadays for a really new idea to be put forward. And any story which depends for its effect on saying to you "Look how clever I am to have thought of this" may fall flat with someone who has read a lot more of them for this reason. Of course this comparative exhaustion of gimmicks and twists was one of the things which led to science-fiction writers having to learn to write better—if the theme could not win simply by its novelty then it just had to be much better written to win at all.

There is, as we have said, a large educated public which knows its literature, and knows nothing of science fiction. We all know how rare it is not to pass judgment on things we know practically nothing about. Up to a point this is fair enough. I personally would agree with Mr. Philip Larkin in thinking that it is a little too much to expect people to force themselves to appreciate new things by making very large efforts. But one feels a certain smug hostility. One sees them clearly, the detractors—whether puffing their Three Nuns over Hugh Walpole in a country vicarage, or lecturing on Henry James in the most advanced jargon. A few years ago the *Observer* held a competition of science-fiction short stories. With one admirable exception (a story by Mr. Brian Aldiss) all the successful stories would have been rejected, and rightly rejected, by any science fiction magazine. The judgment not only showed, presumably, that ignorance of the genre prevails among literary persons who are nevertheless prepared to judge it, but also that literary training produces, not a natural good taste but simply certain conditioned responses, adequate only in familiar fields.

One of the active, rather than merely habitual, misapprehensions about literature can be seen in the thesis put forward frequently and, as might be expected, with the greatest clarity, by Dr. Donald Davie. This is that serious writing can only be done by those who have mastered a cultural syllabus comparable to André Malraux' Imaginary Museum in the visual arts. Even in this general form, the theory seems dubious. Mr. Philip Larkin can write an excellent poem without paying any attention to the writing, or even the existence, of Mr. Ezra Pound. But the particular interpretation given to it consciously by Davie, and implicitly by a large number of those interested, is even less tenable, containing as it does concealed—and faulty—assumptions.

In the first place, it is asserted that an appreciation of foreign literature is a definite requisite. We are told, say, that a certain poet has "assimilated" Laforgue. This sort of claim shows an insensitivity and arrogance which it is hard to understand. The number of English writers who can appreciate French verse as verse must be very few indeed. It may be true that a "fruitful misunderstanding" of a foreign literature is possible, but in that case we can only speak of a stimulus, and one *not* of a "literary" nature. And thus foreign literatures, in general, in so far as they stimulate English literature, are not to be ranked as different in kind from stimuli of a nonliterary type, such as those that science and philosophy may provide. The Imaginary Museum should either be closed down or extended across Exhibition Road to include the Natural History and Science Museums in addition to the V. & A.

In fact, this was always the tradition here until constricting notions about the primacy of Literature and the Human Soul introduced a disproportion into critical and sometimes even creative attitudes. It is not only in science-fiction that there has been something of a return to the principle of Aristotle that character should be subordinate to the story, and, indeed, merely a development of the story. There is plenty of straight fiction which does not follow the tune of the psychological novel. Mr. William Golding, for instance, writes compulsively to his theme. *Lord of the Flies* and *The Inheritors* are both border-line science-fiction novels. It would not have been really surprising to have seen them serialised in *Galaxy*. At the same time the common reader (or even the common critic, more concerned with erecting barriers) is not surprised to see them presented as novels pure and simple. And rightly so. Four hundred years ago imaginative literature was all of a piece. It was not until Aretino that pornography began to become a really specialised job. Shakespeare's characters crack obscene jests in the most natural way between tragic deaths. In the same way, science fiction was part of the ordinary writing of Swift or Voltaire, but until recently it too had long been flourishing as almost a separate cultural tradition. The split in imaginative writing probably took place when a certain type of literary man began to assume, without sufficient reason, that the interplay of "character" was the highest, and then the only, true subject of fictional writing. In recent years much of what used to be regarded as pornographic has been resumed into ordinary literature and there are now reasonable signs that this is happening to science-fiction too. It is difficult to judge whether Samuel Richardson, on reading of a seduction in a spaceship, would have objected more to the act or the venue. We are now, even the specialists, ready for both, I hope.

To conclude on the note I began with: just because science fiction has not been academicised, it is one of the few remaining areas of literature in which reading is done invariably for pleasure and never for duty. It is a case, in fact, of what our attitudes to literature always used to be like. And, one cannot help feeling, of what it is now being increasingly realised they will have to get like again. As Mr. Philip Larkin has written of poetry, "If a poet loses his pleasure-seeking audience he has lost the only audience worth having, for which the dutiful mob that signs on every September is no substitute … if the medium is in fact to be rescued from among our duties and restored to our pleasures, I can only think that a large-scale revulsion has to set in against present notions."

Science fiction illuminates other fields of literature by contrast. But it may be regarded as in some sort an example: a threat or a promise, depending on how you look at it.

The Roots of Science Fiction

by Robert Scholes

All fiction—every book even, fiction or not—takes us out of the world we normally inhabit. To enter a book is to live in another place. Out of the nature of this otherness and its relation to our life experiences come all our theories of interpretation and all our criteria of value. In the previous lecture I argued the case for a particular relation between fiction and experience, expressed in temporal terms as "future-fiction." The polemical nature of my situation as advocate for a popular but critically deprecated form of fiction led me inevitably to make a case which is in certain respects too narrow for its subject. The laws of rhetoric force all radical advocates to choose between betraying their causes by an excess of conciliation or of hostility, and I understand those laws only too well. In compensation, I wish to be more tentative and speculative now, in describing the parameters of a fictional form that is both old and new, rooted in the past but distinctly modern, oriented to the future but not bounded by it.

It is customary in our empirically based Anglo-Saxon criticism to distinguish between two great schools of fiction according to the relationship between the fictional worlds they present and the world of human experience. Thus we have, since the eighteenth century, spoken of novels and romances, of realism and fantasy, and we have found the distinction useful enough at times, even though, because of our empirical bias, we have tended to value realism more highly than romance. It will be appropriate, then, at least as a beginning, to see the tradition that leads to modern science fiction as a special case of romance, for this tradition always insists upon a radical discontinuity between its world and the world of ordinary human

"The Roots of Science Fiction" by Robert Scholes. From *Structural Fabulation: An Essay on Fiction of the Future* (Notre Dame, Indiana: University of Notre Dame Press, 1975), pp. 27–44. Reprinted by permission of University of Notre Dame Press.

experience. In its simplest and most ancient form this discontinuity is objectified as another world, a different place: Heaven, Hell, Eden, Fairyland, Utopia, The Moon, Atlantis, Lilliput. This radical dislocation between the world of romance and the world of experience has been exploited in different ways. One way, the most obvious, has been to suspend the laws of nature in order to give more power to the laws of narrative, which are themselves projections of the human psyche in the form of enacted wishes and fears. These pure enactments are at the root of all narrative structures, are themselves the defining characteristics of all narrative forms, whether found in "realistic" or "fantastic" matrices. In the sublimative narratives of pure romance they are merely more obvious than elsewhere because less disguised by other interests and qualities. But there is another way to exploit the radical discontinuity between the world of romance and that of experience, and this way emphasizes cognition. The difference can be used to get a more vigorous purchase on certain aspects of that very reality which has been set aside in order to generate a romantic cosmos. When romance returns deliberately to confront reality it produces the various forms of didactic romance or fabulation that we usually call allegory, satire, fable, parable, and so on—to indicate our recognition that reality is being addressed indirectly through a patently fictional device.

Fabulation, then, is fiction that offers us a world clearly and radically discontinuous from the one we know, yet returns to confront that known world in some cognitive way. Traditionally, it has been a favorite vehicle for religious thinkers, precisely because religions have insisted that there is more to the world than meets the eye, that the common-sense view of reality—"realism"—is incomplete and therefore false. Science, of course, has been telling us much the same thing for several hundred years. The world we see and hear and feel—"reality" itself—is a fiction of our senses, and dependent on their focal ability, as the simplest microscope will easily demonstrate. Thus it is not surprising that what we call "science" fiction should employ the same narrative vehicle as the religious fictions of our past. In a sense, they are fellow travellers. But there are also great differences between these kinds of fiction, which must be investigated.

There are two varieties of fabulation or didactic romance, which correspond roughly to the distinction between romances of religion and romances of science. We may call these two forms "dogmatic" and "speculative" fabulation, respectively. This distinction is neither complete nor invidious. It represents a tendency rather than delineating a type, but most didactic romances are clearly dominated by one tendency or the other. Even within the Christian tradition, we can recognize Dante's *Commedia* as a dogmatic fabulation and More's *Utopia* as a speculative one. Dante's work is greater by most accepted standards of comparison. But it works out of a closed, anti-speculative system of belief. A *Utopia* admits in its title that it is nowhere. A *Commedia*, human or divine, on the other hand, must fill the known cosmos. As opposed to dogmatic narrative, speculative fabulation is a creature of humanism, associated from its origins with attitudes and values that have shaped the growth of science itself. Swift detested the science of his time, which drove him to dogmatic posturing in Book III of *Gulliver*. But surely without the microscope and telescope Books I and II could not have been as they are. And Book IV is a speculation beyond all dogma. Since Dante, dogmatic fabulation has declined, though it always lurks in the worlds of satire. Since More, speculative fabulation has grown and developed. Born of humanism it has been fostered by science. But it has never flourished as it does at present—for reasons that it is now our business to explore.

As Claudio Guillén has taught us, literature may be usefully seen as aspiring toward system—as a collection of entities constantly rearranging themselves in search of an equilibrium never achieved. In the course of this process certain generic forms crystallize and persist or fade from existence, and among these forms some come into dominance at particular moments of history, only to yield their dominant position with the passage of time. In every age, as the Russian Formalists were fond of observing, certain generic forms are regarded as "canonical"—the accepted forms for the production of serious literature—and other forms are considered outside the pale, being either too esoteric ("coterie literature") or too humble ("popular literature"). But with the passage of time canonical forms become rigid, heavy, mannered, and lose their vital power. Even the dominant forms eventually give up their privileged position and move toward the edges of the literary canon. The reasons for this may be seen in purely formal terms—as the exhaustion of the expressive resources of the genre. Or they may be seen in broader cultural terms—as responses to social or conceptual developments outside the literary system itself. To my way of thinking, since fiction is a cognitive art it cannot be considered adequately in purely formal terms. Formal changes, to be understood, must be seen in the light of other changes in the human situation.

I propose, then, to examine a small but important part of the system of literature: the interaction of certain forms of fictional representation over a period of a few centuries, ending with the present time. And I further propose to see this interaction as an aspect of a larger movement of mind. My treatment will be extremely brief; the model I generate will be very sketchy. But in matters of this kind true persuasion is not to be achieved by the amassing of argumentative detail. I ask you simply to consider the fictional universe from the perspective of this model and then see if your old perspective can ever be comfortably assumed again. I will begin by raising a question seldom considered—perhaps because it is too large to admit of an answer. The question is, simply, "What makes a form dominant?" Admitting the phenomenon of dominance, why, for instance, should drama dominate the western countries of Europe for a hundred years from the late sixteenth through the seventeenth century? In general terms it has been argued, and I think convincingly, that drama was ideally suited to an era in which monolithic feudalism had lost its power over individual existence but bourgeois democracy had not yet come into being as a regulator of the power vacuum left behind by the crumbling feudal system. An age of princes (in the Machiavellian sense) made heroic drama conceivable as neither an earlier age of kings nor a later age of ministers ever could. The dramatic disposition of the age, with its incredible reversals of fortune, as seen, for instance, in the life of an Essex or a Raleigh, enabled a specific literary form to realize its maximum potential.

In the case of the novel, we find a form that came into dominance for parallel cultural reasons. The rise of the middle class did not "cause" the rise of the novel, but new concepts of the human situation enabled both of these phenomena to take place. In particular, a new grasp of history, as a process with its own dynamics resulting from the interaction of social and economic forces, generated a new concept of man as a creature struggling against these impersonal entities. And this struggle could hardly be represented on the stage in the same way as man's struggle with fortune or his own ambitious desires. It is not that plays dealing with socio-economic man could not be written. Writers from Steele to Ibsen struggled manfully to generate a rich social canvas on stage. But what the novel achieved easily and naturally, the drama could do only with great pains and clumsy inadequacy. The novel naturally came to be the literary form in which an age conscious of history as a shaping force could express itself most satisfyingly. The novel was the diachronic form of a diachronic age. In each volume of the great nineteenth-century realists we find the history of an individual against a background of the forces shaping his moment of history. And in the sequences of novels produced by writers like Balzac and Zola we can see whole eras taking human shape, becoming protagonists struggling in the grip of the large designs of History itself. For this, of course, was the age in which History acquired a capital *H,* becoming a substitute for God, with a Grand Purpose in Mind, which His angel the Time-Spirit sought to effect.

Let us narrow the focus, now, to the narrative forms of representation only, for dominance can be considered not only among the great generic kinds, and even among whole arts, but also within the boundaries of a single kind of literature. In the novel itself we can trace the rise and fall from dominance of sentimental fiction in the eighteenth century, of a more sociological and historical fiction in the nineteenth, and finally a more inward and psychological fiction in the early twentieth century. All of these forms have gone under the name of realism, and as an evolving tradition this realism preserved a dominant place among the forms of fiction from the time of Defoe and Marivaux until well into the present century. Other fictional forms have coexisted with the dominant realism—such as the gothic, which first emerged in the late eighteenth century to fill an emotive gap opened in the system by the move of social and sentimental forms away from situations of heroic intensity. And after Swift a speculative fabulation with satirical tendencies was kept alive by writers like Johnson in *Rasselas* and Carlyle in *Sartor Resartus.* But it is fair to say that this tradition lacked vigor and continuity—lacked generic certainty—until new conceptual developments put fictional speculation on an entirely different footing, changing the fabric of man's vision in ways that inevitably led to changes in his fiction.

This revolution in man's conception of himself was begun by Darwin's theory of evolution. It was continued by Einstein's theory of relativity. And it has been extended by developments in the study of human systems of perception, organization, and communication that range from the linguistic philosophy of Wittgenstein and the gestalt psychology of Köhler to the structural anthropology of Lévi-Strauss and the cybernetics of Wiener. This century of cosmic rearrangement, crudely indicated here by this list of names and concepts, has led to new ways of understanding human time and space-time, as well as to a new sense of the relationship between human systems and the larger systems of the cosmos. In its broadest sense, this revolution has replaced Historical Man with Structural Man.

Let us explore this great mental shift a bit. Darwin, and those who have continued his work, put human history in a frame of reference much grander than that of Historical Man. This stretched man's entire sense of time into a new shape and finally altered his familiar position in the cosmos. Early reactions to evolutionary theory often tried to accommodate Darwinian evolutionary theory within the familiar dimensions of historical time, suggesting that some Superman lurked just around the evolutionary corner—in much the same way that people once believed the apocalypse to be scheduled for the very near future. But by expanding our sense of time the Darwinians reduced history to a moment and man to a bit player in a great unfinished narrative. The possibility of further evolution, with species more advanced than ourselves coming into being on this earth, displaced man from the final point of traditional cosmic teleology as effectively as Galileo had displaced man's planet from the center of the spatial cosmos. Thus Darwinian time, which has been continually extended with the discovery of new geological and archeological evidence, has had a profound effect on man's sense of himself and his possibilities. Historical time, then, is only a tiny fragment of human time, which is again a tiny fragment of geologic time, which is itself only a bit of cosmic time.

The theories of relativity have worked in a similar fashion to shake man out of his humanist perspective. By demonstrating that space and time are in a more intimate perspectival relation than we had known, Einstein too called history into question. When we think in terms of the cosmic distances and absolute velocities of the Einsteinian universe, not only do we lose our grasp on fundamental human concepts like "simultaneity" and "identity," we lose also our confidence in that commonsense apprehension of the world which replaced man's mythic consciousness as the novel replaced the epic in the hierarchy of narrative forms. And on the smaller scale of purely human studies in anthropology, psychology, and linguistics, ideas no less earth-shaking have been developed. What does it do to our time sense to think of stone-age men living their timeless lives in the year 1974 in some remote jungle on our earth? And what does it do to our confidence in human progress when we see that though they lack all the things that our science and technology have given us, they live in a harmony with the cosmos that shames us, and know instinctively, it seems, lessons that we are painfully relearning by having to face the consequences of our own ecological wantonness? At every turn we run into patterns of shaping force that have gone unobserved by our instrumental approach to the world. We learn that men's visual perceptions are governed by mental leaps to whole configurations or "gestalts" rather than by patient accumulation of phenomenal details. We learn that we acquire language in similar quantum jumps of grammatical competence. And we know that our acquired languages in turn govern and shape our perceptions of this world. Finally, we have begun to perceive that our social systems and our linguistic systems share certain similarities of pattern, that even our most intimate forms of behavior are ordered by behavioral configurations beyond our perception and controlled through biological feed-back systems that may be altered by the input of various drugs, hormones, and other biochemical messages.

In short, we are now so aware of the way that our lives are part of a patterned universe that we are free to speculate as never before. Where anything may be true—sometime, someplace—there can be no heresy. And where the patterns of the cosmos itself guide our thoughts so powerfully, so beautifully, we have nothing to fear but our own lack of courage. There are fields of force around us that even our finest instruments of thought and perception are only beginning to detect. The job of fiction is to play in these fields. And in the past few decades fiction has begun to do just this, to dream new dreams, confident that there is no gate of ivory, only a gate of horn, and that all dreams are true. It is fiction—verbal narrative—that must take the lead in such dreaming, because even the new representational media that have been spawned in this age cannot begin to match the speculative agility and imaginative freedom of words. The camera can capture only what is found in front of it or made for it, but language is as swift as thought itself and can reach beyond what is, or seems, to what may or may not be, with the speed of a synapse. Until the mind can speak in its own tongueless images, the word will be its fleetest and most delicate instrument of communication. It is not strange, then, that the modern revolution in human thought should find expression in a transformation of a form of fictional speculation that has been available for centuries. It took only a quantum jump in fictional evolution for speculative fabulation to become structural, and the mutation took place some time early in this century.

What, then, is structural fabulation? ... Considered generically, structural fabulation is simply a new mutation in the tradition of speculative fiction. It is the tradition of More, Bacon, and Swift, as modified by new input from the physical and human sciences. Considered as an aspect of the whole system of contemporary fiction, it has grown in proportion to the decline of other fictional forms. For instance, to the extent that the dominant realistic novel has abandoned the pleasures of narrative movement for the cares of psychological and social analysis, a gap in the system has developed which a number of lesser forms have sought to fill. All the forms of adventure fiction, from western, to detective, to spy, to costume— have come into being in response to the movement of "serious" fiction away from plot and the pleasures of fictional sublimation. Because many human beings experience a psychological need for narration—whether cultural or biological in origin—the literary system *must* include works which answer to that need. But when the dominant canonical form fails to satisfy such a basic drive, the system becomes unbalanced. The result is that readers resort secretly and guiltily to lesser forms for that narrative fix they cannot do without. And many feel nearly as guilty about it as we could hope to make any habitual offender against our official mores. The spectacle (reported by George Moore, as I recollect) of W. B. Yeats explaining with great embarrassment why he happened to be reading a detective story can stand as a paradigm of the guilt felt by intellectuals whose emotional needs drive them to lesser literary forms for pleasure. We do call people "addicts" if they seem inordinately fond of detective stories, or even of science fiction. But the metaphor of addiction is a dangerously misleading one. For this is emotional food, not a mind-bending narcotic, that we are considering.

Thus the vacuum left by the movement of "serious" fiction away from storytelling has been filled by "popular" forms with few pretensions to any virtues beyond those of narrative excitement. But the very emptiness of these forms, as they are usually managed, has left another gap, for forms which supply readers' needs for narration without starving their needs for intellection. The "letdown" experienced after finishing many detective stories or adventure tales comes from a sense of time wasted—time in which we have deliberately suspended not merely our sense of disbelief but also far too many of our normal cognitive processes. And this letdown grows to a genuine and appropriate feeling of guilt to the extent that we *do* become addicted and indulge in the reading of such stories beyond our normal need for diversion and sublimation. Even food should not be taken in abnormal quantities, especially if much of it is empty calories. We require a fiction which satisfies our cognitive and sublimative needs together, just as we want food which tastes good and provides some nourishment. We need suspense with intellectual consequences, in which questions are raised as well as solved, and in which our minds are expanded even while focused on the complications of a fictional plot.

These may be described as our general requirements—needs which have existed as long as man has been sufficiently civilized to respond to a form that combines sublimation and cognition. But we also have to consider here the special requirements of our own age—our need for fictions which provide a sublimation relevant to the specific conditions of being in which we find ourselves. The most satisfying fictional response to these needs takes the form of what may be called structural fabulation. In works of structural fabulation the tradition of speculative fiction is modified by an awareness of the nature of the universe as a system of systems, a structure of structures, and the insights of the past century of science are accepted as fictional points of departure. Yet structural fabulation is neither scientific in its methods nor a substitute for actual science. It is a fictional exploration of human situations made perceptible by the implications of recent science. Its favorite themes involve the impact of developments or revelations derived from the human or the physical sciences upon the people who must live with those revelations or developments.

In the previous era, historicist views of human culture led to a vision of man's future as guided by some plan beyond human comprehension, perhaps, in its totality, but solicitous of man and amenable to human cooperation. Thus great fictional narratives could be couched in terms of individual men and women seeking to align themselves with or struggle against the social forces through which History was working its Will to achieve its Idea. But now structuralism dominates our thought, with its view of human existence as a random happening in a world which is orderly in its laws but without plan or purpose. Thus man must learn to live within laws that have given him his being but offer him no purpose and promise him no triumph as a species. Man must make his own values, fitting his hopes and fears to a universe which has allowed him a place in its systematic working, but which cares only for the system itself and not for him. Man must create his future himself. History will not do it for him. And the steps he has already taken to modify the biosphere can be seen as limiting the future options of the human race. It is in this atmosphere that structural fabulation draws its breath, responding to these conditions of being, in the form of extrapolative narrative. The extrapolations may be bold and philosophical or cautious and sociological, but they must depart from what we know and consider what we have due cause to hope and fear. Like all speculative fabulations they will take their origin in some projected dislocation of our known existence, but their projections will be based on a contemporary apprehension of the biosphere as an ecosystem and the universe as a cosmosystem.

Obviously, not all works that are called "science fiction" meet this kind of standard. Many writers are so deficient in their understanding of the cosmic structure itself that they have no sense of the difference between purposeful discontinuity and a magical relaxation of the cosmic structure. And many others seek to present traditional romance as if it had some structural or speculative significance. But, if a writer fails to understand the discontinuity on which his work is based *as* a discontinuity *from* a contemporary view of what is true or natural, he is powerless to make that discontinuity function structurally for us. Thus any cognitive thrust in his work will be accidental and intermittent. And if a writer transports men to Mars merely to tell a cowboy story, he produces not structural fabulation but star dreck—harmless, perhaps, but an abuse of that economy of means that governs mature esthetic satisfaction. Or if he allows such a variety of magical events that his fictional world seems deficient in its own natural laws, his work will fail structurally and cognitively, too, though it may retain some sublimative force. But in the most admirable of structural fabulations, a radical discontinuity between the fictional world and our own provides both the means of narrative suspense and of speculation. In the perfect structural fabulation, idea and story are so wedded as to afford us simultaneously the greatest pleasures that fiction provides: sublimation and cognition.

On the Poetics of the
Science Fiction Genre

by Darko Suvin[1]

1. Science Fiction As Fiction (Estrangement)

1.1. The importance of science fiction (SF) in our time is on the increase. First, there are strong indications that its popularity in the leading industrial nations (USA, USSR, UK, Japan) has risen sharply over the last 100 years, regardless of local and short-range fluctuations. SF has particularly affected some key strata of modern society such as the college graduates, young writers, and the avant garde of general readers appreciative of new sets of values. This is a significant cultural effect which goes beyond any merely quantitative census. Second, if one takes as minimal generic differences of SF either *radically different figures* (dramatis personae) or a *radically different context* of the story, it will be found to have an interesting and close kinship with other literary sub-genres, which flourished at different times and places of literary history: the Greek and Hellenistic "blessed island" stories, the "fabulous voyage" from Antiquity on, the Renaissance and Baroque "utopia" and "planetary novel," the Enlightenment "state (political) novel," the modern "anticipation," "anti-utopia," etc. Moreover, although SF

"On the Poetics of the Science Fiction Genre" by Darko Suvin. From *College English*, XXXIV (December, 1972), 372–83. Copyright © 1972 by the National Council of Teachers of English. Reprinted by permission of the publisher and the author.

[1] The first version of this essay crystallized out of a lecture given in J. M. Holquist's seminar on fantastic literature in the Yale University Slavic Department in Spring, 1968. It was first published in *College English*, where many other debts are mentioned, and in lieu of elaborate annotation, a now somewhat dated bibliography of the most prominent books on SF is included. I should like here to record particularly my gratitude to the Canada Council, whose research grants helped to shape its final form. "Literature" and "literary" in this essay are synonymous with "fiction" and "fictional."

shares with myth, fantasy, fairy tale and pastoral an opposition to
naturalistic or empiricist literary genres, it differs very significantly
in approach and social function from such adjoining non-naturalistic or meta-empirical genres. Both of these complementary aspects,
the sociological and the methodological, are being vigorously
debated among writers and critics in several countries; both testify
to the relevance of this genre and the need of scholarly discussion
too.

In the following paper I shall argue for a definition of SF as the
literature of cognitive estrangement. This definition seems to possess the
unique advantage of rendering justice to a literary tradition which
is coherent through the ages and within itself, and yet distinct from
non-fictional utopianism, from naturalistic literature, and from
other non-naturalistic fiction. It thus permits us to lay the basis of a
coherent poetics of SF.

1.2. I should like to approach such a discussion, and this field of
discourse, by postulating a spectrum or spread of literary subject-
matter, running from the ideal extreme of exact recreation of the
author's empirical environment[2] to exclusive interest in a strange

---

[2] A virtue of discussing this seemingly peripheral subject of "science fiction" and
its "utopian" tradition is that one has to go back to first principles, one cannot
really assume them as given—such as in this case what is literature. Usually, when
discussing literature one determines what it says (its subject matter) and how it
says what it says (the approach to its themes). If we are talking about literature in
the sense of significant works possessing certain minimal aesthetic qualities rather
than in the sociological sense of everything that gets published at a certain time or
the ideological sense of all the writings on certain themes, this principle can more
precisely be formulated as a double question. First, epistemologically, what
possibility for aesthetic qualities is offered by different thematic fields ("subjects")?
The answer of dominant aesthetics at the moment is—an absolutely equal
possibility, and with this answer our aesthetics kicks the question out of its field
into the lap of ideologists who pick it up by default and proceed to bungle it.
Second, historically, how has such a possibility in fact been used? Once you begin
with such considerations you come quickly up against the rather unclear concept
of *realism* (not the prose literary movement in the 19th century but a meta-histori-
cal stylistic principle), since the SF genre is often pigeonholed as non-realistic. I
would not object but would heartily welcome such labels if one had first
persuasively defined what is "real" and what is "reality." True, this genre raises
basic philosophical issues; but it is perhaps not necessary to face them in a first
approach. Therefore I shall here substitute for "realism" and "reality" the concept
of "the author's empirical environment," which seems as immediately clear as any.

newness, a *novum*. From the eighteenth to the twentieth century, the literary mainstream of our civilization has been nearer to the first of the two above-mentioned extremes. However, at the beginnings of a literature, the concern with a domestication of the amazing is very strong. Early tale-tellers tell about amazing voyages into the next valley where they found dog-headed people, also good rock salt which could be stolen or at the worst bartered for. Their stories are a syncretic travelog and *voyage imaginaire*, daydream and intelligence report. This implies a curiosity about the unknown beyond the next mountain range (sea, ocean, solar system ...), where the thrill of knowledge joined the thrill of adventure.

An island in the far-off ocean is the paradigm of the aesthetically most satisfying goal of the SF voyage, from Iambulus and Euhemerus through the classical utopia to Verne's island of Captain Nemo and Wells' island of Dr. Moreau; especially if we subsume under this the planetary island in the aether ocean—usually the Moon—from Lucian through Cyrano and Swift's mini-Moon of Laputa to the 19th century. Yet the parallel paradigm of the valley, "over the range" [3] which shuts it in as a wall, is perhaps as revealing. It recurs almost as frequently, from the earliest folk tales about the sparkling valley of Terrestrial Paradise and the dark valley of the Dead, both already in *Gilgamesh*. Eden is the mythological localization of utopian longing, just as Wells' valley in the *Country of the Blind* is still within the liberating tradition which contends that the world is not necessarily the way our present empirical valley happens to be, and that whoever thinks his valley is the world, is blind. Whether island or valley, whether in space or (from the industrial and bourgeois revolutions on) in time, the new framework is correlative to the new inhabitants. The aliens—utopians, monsters or simple differing strangers—are a mirror to man just as the differing country is a mirror for his world. But the mirror is not only a reflecting one, it is also a transforming one, virgin womb and alchemical dynamo: the mirror is a crucible.

Thus, it is not only the basic human and humanizing curiosity that gives birth to SF. Beside an undirected inquisitiveness, a semantic game without clear referent, this genre has always been wedded to a hope of finding in the unknown the ideal environment,

[3] Sub-title of Samuel Butler's SF novel *Erewhon*.

tribe, state, intelligence or other aspect of the Supreme Good (or to a fear of and revulsion from its contrary). At all events, the *possibility* of other strange, co-variant coordinate systems and semantic fields is assumed.

1.3. The approach to the imaginary locality, or localized day-dream, practiced by the genre of SF is a supposedly factual one. Columbus' (technically or genologically non-fictional) letter on the Eden he glimpsed beyond the Orinoco mouth, and Swift's (technically non-factual) voyage to "Laputa, Balnibarbi, Glubbdubbdrib, Luggnagg *and Japan*," stand at the opposite ends of a constant interpenetration of imaginary and empirical possibilities. Thus SF takes off from a fictional ("literary") hypothesis and develops it with extrapolating and totalizing ("scientific") rigor—the specific difference between Columbus and Swift is smaller than their generic proximity. The effect of such factual reporting of fictions is one of confronting a set normative system—a Ptolemaic-type closed world picture—with a point of view or glance implying a new set of norms; in literary theory, this is known as the attitude of *estrangement.* This concept was first developed on non-naturalistic texts by the Russian Formalists ("ostranenie," Viktor Shklovsky 1917), and most successfully underpinned by an anthropological and historical approach in the opus of Bertolt Brecht, who wanted to write "plays for a scientific age." While working on a play about the prototype scientist Galileo, he defined this attitude ("Verfremdungseffekt") in his *Short Organon for the Theatre* (1948): "A representation which estranges is one which allows us to recognize its subject, but at the same time makes it seem unfamiliar." And further: for somebody to see all normal happenings in a dubious light, "he would need to develop that detached eye with which the great Galileo observed a swinging chandelier. He was amazed by the pendulum motion as if he had not expected it and could not understand its occurring, and this enabled him to come at the rules by which it was governed." Thus, the look of estrangement is both cognitive and creative; and as Brecht goes on to say: "one cannot simply exclaim that such an attitude pertains to science, but not to art. Why should not art, in its own way, try to serve the great social task of mastering Life?" [4] (Later, Brecht was also to note it might be

[4] Viktor Shklovsky, "Iskusstvo kak priem," in *Poètika*, Petrograd, 1919. In the English translation of this essay "Art as Technique," in Lee T. Lemon and Marion

time to stop speaking in terms of masters and servants altogether.)

In SF, the attitude of estrangement—used by Brecht in a different way, within a still predominantly "realistic" context—has grown into the *formal framework* of the genre.

2. *Science Fiction As Cognition (Critique and Science)*

2.1. The use of estrangement both as underlying attitude and dominant formal device is found also in the *myth*, a ritual and religious approach looking in its own way beneath the empiric surface. However, SF sees the norms of any age, including emphatically its own, as unique, changeable, and therefore subject to a *cognitive* glance. The myth is diametrically opposed to the cognitive approach since it conceives human relations as fixed, and supernaturally determined, emphatically denying Montaigne's: "la constance même n'est qu'un branle plus languissant." The myth absolutizes and even personifies apparently constant motifs from the sluggish periods with low social dynamics. Conversely, SF, which is organized by extrapolating the variable and future-bearing elements from the empirical environment, clusters in the great whirlpool periods of history, such as the 16–17th and 19–20th century. Where the myth claims to explain once and for all the essence of phenomena, SF posits them first as problems and then explores where they lead to; it sees the mythical static identity as an illusion, usually as fraud, in the best case only as a temporary realization of potentially limitless contingencies. It does not ask about The Man or The World, but which man?: in which kind of

J. Reis eds., *Russian Formalist Criticism: Four Essays*, Lincoln, Nebraska, 1965, *ostranenie* is rendered somewhat clumsily as "defamiliarization." Cf. also the illuminating survey of Victor Erlich, *Russian Formalism: History-Doctrine*, The Hague, 1955.

Bertolt Brecht, "Kleines Organon für das Theater," in his *Schriften zum Theater 7*, Frankfurt, 1964, transl. in John Willett ed., *Brecht On Theatre*, New York, 1964. My quotations are from p. 192 and 96 of this translation, in which I have changed Mr. Willett's translation of Verfremdung as "alienation" into my "estrangement," since alienation evokes incorrect, indeed opposite connotations: estrangement was for Brecht an approach militating directly against social and cognitive alienation —see Ernst Bloch, "*Entfremdung, Verfremdung*: Alienation, Estrangement," in Erika Munk, ed., *Brecht*, New York, 1972.

world?: and why such a man in such kind of world? As a literary genre, SF is just as opposed to supernatural or metaphysical estrangement as to empiricism (naturalism).

2.2. *SF is, then, a literary genre whose necessary and sufficient conditions are the presence and interaction of estrangement and cognition, and whose main formal device is an imaginative framework alternative to the author's empirical environment.*

The estrangement differentiates it from the "realistic" literary mainstream of 18th to 20th century. The cognition differentiates it not only from myth, but also from the fairy tale and the fantasy. The *fairy tale* also doubts the laws of the author's empirical world, but it escapes out of its horizons and into a closed collateral world indifferent toward cognitive possibilities. It does not use imagination as a means to understand the tendencies in reality, but as an end sufficient unto itself and cut off from the real contingencies. The stock fairy-tale accessory, such as the flying carpet, evades the empirical law of physical gravity—as the hero evades social gravity—by imagining its opposite. The wishfulfilling element is its strength and weakness, for it never pretends that a carpet could be expected to fly—that a humble third son could be expected to become a king—while there is gravity. It just posits another world beside yours where some carpets do, magically, fly, and some paupers do, magically, become princes, and into which you cross purely by an act of faith and fancy. Anything is possible in a fairy tale, because a fairy tale is manifestly impossible. Therefore, SF retrogressing into fairy tale (e.g. a "space opera" with a hero-prin-cess-monster triangle in astronautic costume) is committing creative suicide.

Even less congenial to SF is the *fantasy* (ghost, horror, Gothic, weird) tale, a genre committed to the interposition of anti-cognitive laws into the empirical environment. Where the fairy tale was indifferent, the fantasy is inimical to the empirical world and its laws. The thesis could be defended that the fantasy is significant insofar as it is impure and fails to establish a super-ordinated maleficent world of its own, causing a grotesque tension between arbitrary supernatural phenomena and the empirical norms they infiltrate into. Gogol's Nose is so interesting because it is walking down the Nevski Prospect, with a certain rank in the civil service, etc.; if the Nose were in a completely fantastic world—say H. P.

Lovecraft's—it would be just another ghoulish thrill. When fantasy does not make for such a tension between its norms and the author's empirical environment, its reduction of all possible horizons to Death makes of it just a sub-literature of mystification. Commercial lumping of it into the same category as SF is thus a grave disservice and rampantly socio-pathological phenomenon.

2.3. As different from such harsh but deserved words, the *pastoral* is essentially closer to SF. Its imaginary framework of a world without money economy, state apparatus, and depersonalizing urbanization allows it to isolate, as in laboratory, two human motivations—erotics and power-hunger. This approach relates to SF as alchemy does to chemistry and nuclear physics: an early try in the right direction with insufficient sophistication. SF has thus much to learn from the pastoral tradition, primarily from its directly sensual relationships without class alienation. It has in fact often done so, whenever it has sounded the theme of the triumph of the humble (Restif, Morris, etc. up to Simak, Christopher, Yefremov, Le Guin ...). Unfortunately, the Baroque pastoral abandoned this theme and jelled into a sentimental convention, discrediting the genre; but when the pastoral escapes preciosity, its hope can fertilize the SF field as an antidote to pragmatism, commercialism, other-directedness and technocracy.

2.4. Claiming a Galilean or Brunoan estrangement for SF does not at all mean committing it to scientific vulgarization or even technological prognostication, which it was engaged in at various times (some Verne, U.S. in the 1920's–1930's, U.S.S.R. under Stalinism). The needful and meritorious task of popularization can be a useful element of the SF works at a juvenile level. But even the *"roman scientifique"* such as Verne's *From the Earth to the Moon*—or the surface level of Wells' *Invisible Man*—though a legitimate SF form, is a lower stage in its development. It is very popular with audiences just approaching SF, such as the juvenile, because it introduces into the old empirical context only *one* easily digestible new technological variable (Moon missile, or rays which lower the refractive index of organic matter).[5] The euphoria provoked by this apporach is real

[5] Note the functional difference to the anti-gravity metal in Wells' *First Man on the Moon*, which is an introductory gadget and not the be-all of a much richer novel.

but limited, better suited to the short story and a new audience. It evaporates much quicker as the positivistic natural science loses prestige in the humanistic sphere after the World Wars (cf. Nemo's as against the U.S. Navy's atomic "Nautilus"), and surges back with prestigious peace-time applications in new methodologies (astronautics, cybernetics). Even in Verne, the structure of the "science novel" is that of a pond after a stone has been thrown into it: there is a momentary commotion, the waves go from impact point to periphery and back, then the system settles down as before. The only difference is that one positivistic fact—usually an item of hardware—has been added, like the stone to the pond bottom. This structure of transient estrangement is specific to murder mysteries, not to a mature SF.

2.5. After such delimitations, it is perhaps possible at least to indicate some differentiations within the concept of "cognitiveness" or "cognition." As used here, this term does not imply only a reflecting *of* but also *on* reality. It implies a creative approach tending toward a dynamic transformation rather than toward a static mirroring of the author's environment. Such typical methodology of SF—from Lucian, More, Rabelais, Cyrano, and Swift to Wells, London, Zamiatin and the last decades—is a *critical* one, often satirical, combining a belief in the potentialities of reason with methodical doubt in the most significant cases. The kinship of this cognitive critique with the philosophical fundaments of modern science is evident.

3. Science Fiction as a Literary Genre (Functions and Models)

3.0. As a full-fledged literary genre, SF has its own repertory of functions, conventions and devices. Many of them are highly interesting and significant for literary theory and history, but their range can scarcely be discussed in a brief approach as it is properly the subject for a book-length work. However, it might be possible to sketch some determining parameters of the genre.

3.1. In a typology of literary genres for our cognitive age,[6] one

---

[6] I have tried to develop such a typology somewhat more fully in the essay "Science Fiction and the Genological Jungle," *Genre* 6, No. 3 (Sept. 1973).

basic parameter would take into account the relationship of the world(s) each genre presents and the "zero world" of empirically verifiable properties around the author (this being "zero" in the sense of a central reference point in a coordinate system, or of the control group in an experiment). Let us call this empirical world *naturalistic* (though we could have also called it "realistic," "mundane," "this-worldly" etc.). In it, and in the corresponding "naturalistic" literature, ethics are in no significant relation to physics. Modern mainstream literature is forbidden the pathetic fallacy of earthquakes announcing the assassination of rulers or drizzles accompanying the sadness of the heroine. It is the activity of the protagonists, interacting with other, physically equally unprivileged figures, that determines the outcome. However superior technologically or sociologically one side in the conflict may be, any predetermination as to its outcome is felt as an ideological imposition and genological impurity:[7] the basic rule of naturalistic literature is that man's destiny is man, i.e., other humans. On the contrary, in non-naturalistic, *metaphysical* literary genres, discussed in 2.1 and 2.2, circumstances around the hero are neither passive nor neutral. The fairy-tale world is oriented positively toward its protagonist. A fairy tale is defined by the hero's triumph: magic weapons and helpers are, with necessary narrative retardations, at his beck and call. Inversely, the world of the tragic myth is oriented negatively toward its protagonist. Oedipus, Attis or Christ are predestined to empirical failure by the nature of their world—but the failure is then ethically exalted and recuperated for religious use. The fantasy—a derivation of the tragic myth just as the fairy tale derives from the victorious hero myth—is defined by the hero's horrible helplessness: it can be thought of as tragic mythemes without metaphysical compensations. Thus, in the fairy tale and

[7] In cases such as some novels of Hardy and plays by Ibsen, or some of the more doctrinaire works of the historical school of Naturalism, where determinism strongly stresses circumstances at the expense of the main figures' activity, we have underneath a surface appearance of "realism" obviously to do with a bourgeois approach to tragic myth using a shamefaced motivation in an unbelieving age. As contrary to Shakespeare and the Romantics, in this case ethics follow physics in a supposedly causal chain (most often through biology). An analogous approach to fairy tales is to be found in, say, the mimicry of "realism" found in the Hollywood happy-end movies.

the fantasy ethics coincide with (positive or negative) physics, in the tragic myth they compensate the physics, in the "optimistic" myth they supply the coincidence with a systematic framework.

The world of a work of SF is not *a priori* intentionally oriented toward its protagonists, either positively or negatively; the protagonists may succeed or fail in their objectives, but nothing in their basic contrast with the reader, in the physical laws of their worlds, guarantees either. SF is thus (possibly with the exception of some prefigurations in the pastoral) the only meta-empirical genre which is not at the same time metaphysical; it shares with the dominant literature of our civilization a mature approach analogous to that of modern science and philosophy. Furthermore, it shares the omni-temporal horizons of such an approach. The myth is located above time, the fairy tale in a conventional grammatical past which is really outside time, and the fantasy in the hero's abnormally disturbed present. The naturalistic literary mainstream and SF can range through all times: empirical ones in the first, non-empirical ones in the latter case. The naturalistic literary mainstream concentrates on the present, but it can deal with the historical past, and even to some degree with the future in the form of hopes, fears, premonitions, dreams, *et sim.* SF concentrates on possible futures and their spatial equivalents, but it can deal with the present and the past as special cases of a possible historical sequence seen from an estranged point of view (by a figure from another time and/or space). SF can thus use the creative potentialities of an approach not limited by a consuming concern with empirical surfaces and relationships.

3.2. As a matter of historical record, SF started from a pre-scientific or proto-scientific approach of debunking satire and naive social critique, and moved closer to the increasingly sophisticated natural and human sciences. The natural sciences caught up and surpassed the literary imagination in the 19th century; the sciences dealing with human relationships might be argued to have caught up with it in their highest theoretical achievements but have certainly not done so in their alienated social practice. In the 20th century, SF has moved into the sphere of anthropological and cosmological thought, becoming a diagnosis, a warning, a call to understanding and action, and—most important—a mapping of possible alternatives. This historical movement of SF can be envisaged as an enrichment of and shift from a basic direct or extrapolative model to an indirect or analogic model.

3.3. The earlier dominant model of SF from the 19th century on (though not necessarily in preceding epochs) was one which started from certain cognitive hypotheses and ideas incarnated in the fictional framework and nucleus of the fable. This *extrapolative model*—e.g., of London's *Iron Heel*, Wells' *The Sleeper Wakes* and *Men Like Gods*, Zamiatin's *We*, Stapledon's *Last and First Men*, Pohl and Kornbluth's *Space Merchants*, or Yefremov's *Andromeda*—is based on direct, temporal extrapolation and centered on sociological (i.e., utopian and anti-utopian) modelling. This is where the great majority of the "new maps of hell" belongs for which postwar SF is justly famous, in all its manifold combinations of socio-technological scientific cognition and anti-cognitive social oppression (global catastrophes, cybernetic take-overs, dictatorships). Yet already in Wells' *Time Machine* and in Stapledon, this extrapolation transcended the sociological spectrum (from everyday practice through economics to erotics) and spilled into biology and cosmology. Nonetheless, whatever its ostensible location (future, "fourth dimension," other planets, alternative universes), extrapolative modelling is oriented futurologically. Its values and standards are to be found in the cognitive import of the fable's premises and the consistency with which such premises (usually one or very few in number) are narratively developed to its logical end, to a cognitively significant conclusion.

SF can thus be used as a handmaiden of futurological foresight in technology, ecology, sociology, etc. Whereas this may be a legitimate secondary function the genre can be made to bear, any oblivion of its strict secondariness usually leads to confusion and indeed danger. Ontologically, art is not pragmatic truth nor fiction fact. To expect from SF more than a stimulus for independent thinking, more than a system of stylized narrative devices understandable only by way of their mutual relationships within a fictional whole and not as isolated realities, leads insensibly to critical demand for and of scientific accuracy in the extrapolated *realia*. Editors and publishers of such "hard" persuasion have, from the U.S. pulp magazines to the Soviet agitprop, been inclined to turn the handmaiden of SF into the slavery of the reigning theology of the day (technocratic, psionic, utopian, catastrophic, or whatever). Yet this fundamentally subversive genre languishes in strait-jackets more quickly than most other ones, responding with atrophy, escapism, or both. Laying no claim to prophecies except for its statistically to be expected share, SF should not be treated as a prophet: neither enthroned when apparently successful, nor beheaded when apparently unsuccessful. As Plato found out in the court of Dionysus and Hythloday at cardinal Morton's, SF figures better devote themselves to their own literary republics; which, to be sure, lead back—but in their own way—to the Republic of Man. SF is finally concerned with the tensions between *Civitas Dei* and *Civitas Terrena*, and it cannot be uncritically committed to any mundane City.

3.4. The *analogic model* in SF is based on analogy rather than extrapolation. Its figures may but do not have to be anthropomorphic or its localities geomorphic. The objects, figures, and up to a point the relationships from which this indirectly modelled world starts can be quite fantastic (in the sense of empirically unverifiable) as long as they are logically, philosophically and mutually consistent. Again, as in all distinctions of this essay, one should think of a continuum at whose extremes there is pure extrapolation and analogy, and of two fields grouped around the poles and shading into each other on a wide front in the middle.

The lowest form of analogic modelling goes back to a region where distinction between a crude analogy and an extrapolation backwards are not yet distinguishable: it is the analogy to Earth past, from geological through biological to ethnological and historical. The worlds more or less openly modelled on the Carboniferous Age, on tribal prehistory, on barbaric and feudal empires—in fact modelled on handbooks of geology and anthropology, on Spengler and *The Three Musketeers*—are unfortunately abundant in the foothills of SF. Some of them may be useful adolescent leisure reading, which one should not begrudge; however, their uneasy coexistence with a superscience in the story framework or around the protagonist, which is supposed to provide an SF alibi, brings them close to or over the brink of minimum cognitive standards required. The Burroughs-to-Asimov space-opera, cropping up in almost all U.S. writers right down to Samuel Delany belongs here, i.e., into the uneasy borderline between inferior SF and non-SF (forms mimicking SF scenery but modelled on the structures of the Western and other avatars of fairy tale and fantasy).

The highest form of analogic modelling would be the analogy to a mathematical model, such as the fairly primary one explicated in Abbott's *Flatland*, as well as the ontological analogies found in a compressed overview form in some stories by Borges and the Polish writer Lem, and in a somewhat more humane narration with a suffering protagonist in some stories by Kafka (*The Metamorphosis* or *In the Penal Colony*) and novels by Lem (*Solaris*). Such highly sophisticated philosophico-anthropological analogies are today perhaps the most significant region of SF, indistinguishable in quality from the best mainstream writing. Situated between Borges and the upper reaches into which shade the best utopias, anti-utopias and satires, this semantic field is a modern variant of the *conte philosophique* of the 18th century. Similar to Swift, Voltaire, or Diderot, these *modern parables* fuse new vision of the world with an applicability—usually satirical and grotesque—to the shortcomings of our workaday world. As different from the older Rationalism, a modern parable must be open-ended by analogy to modern cosmology, epistemology, philosophy of science, and indeed liberating politics.[8]

The indirect models of SF fall, however, still clearly within its cognitive horizons insofar as their conclusions or import is concerned. The cognition gained may not be immediately applicable, it may be simply the enabling of the mind to receive new wavelengths, but it eventually contributes to the understanding of the most mundane matters. This is testified by the works of Kafka and Lem, of Karel Čapek and Anatole France, as well as of the best of Wells and the "SF reservation" writers.

4. For a Poetics of Science Fiction (Summation and Anticipation)

4.1. The above sketch should, no doubt, be supplemented by a sociological analysis of the "inner environment" of SF, exiled since

---

[8] I have tried to analyze two such representative works in my afterword to Stanislaw Lem's *Solaris*, New York, 1970 and 1971, entitled "The Open-Ended Parables of Stanislaw Lem and *Solaris*," and in my "Introduction" to Karel Čapek's *War With the Newts*, Boston, 1975.

the beginning of the 20th century into a reservation or ghetto which was protective and is now constrictive, cutting off new developments from healthy competition and the highest critical standards. Such a sociological discussion would enable us to point out the important differences between the highest reaches of the genre, glanced at in this essay in order to define functions and standards of SF, and the 80 percent or more of debilitating confectionery. Yet it should be stressed that, as different from many other para-literary genres, the criteria for the insufficiency of most SF are to be found in the genre itself. This makes SF in principle, if not yet in practice, equivalent to any other "major" literary genre.

4.2. If the whole above argumentation is found acceptable, it will be possible to supplement it also by a survey of forms and sub-genres. Beside some mentioned in 1.1. which recur in an updated garb—such as the utopia and fabulous voyage—sub-genres or forms such as the anticipation, the superman story, the artificial intelligence (robots, androids, etc.) story, time-travel, catastrophe or meeting with aliens would have to be analyzed. The various sub-genres of SF could then be checked for their relationships to other literary genres, to each other, and to various sciences. For example, the utopias are—whatever else they may be—clearly sociological fictions or social-science-fiction,[9] whereas modern SF is analogous to modern polycentric cosmology, uniting time and space in Einsteinian worlds with different but co-variant dimensions and time scales. Significant modern SF, with deeper and more lasting sources of enjoyment, also presupposes more complex and wider cognitions: it discusses primarily the political, psychological, an-thropological *use and effect of cognition (natural sciences, human sciences, and philosophy of science), and the becoming or failure of new realities as a result of it.* The consistency of extrapolation, precision of analogy and width of reference in such a cognitive discussion turn into aesthetic factors. (That is why the "scientific novel" discussed in 2.3. is not felt as completely satisfactory—it is aesthetically poor because it is scientifically meager.) Once the elastic criteria of literary structur-ing have been met, *a cognitive—in most cases strictly scientific—element*

---

[9] See further argumentation in my essays "Defining the Literary Genre of Utopia," *Studies in the Literary Imagination* 6, No. 2 (Fall 1973), and "The River-Side Trees, or SF & Utopia," *The Minnesota Review*, n.s., No. 2–3 (Spring–Fall 1974).

becomes a measure of aesthetic quality, of the specific pleasure to be sought in SF. In other words, the cognitive nucleus of the plot co-determines the fictional estrangement in SF. This works on all literary levels: e.g., purely aesthetic, story-telling reasons led modern SF to the cognitive assumption of a hyperspace where flight speed is not limited by the speed of light.

4.3. Finally, it might be possible to sketch the basic premises of a significant criticism, history and theory of this literary genre. From Edgar Allan Poe to Damon Knight, including some notable work on the older sub-genres from the utopias to Wells, and some general approaches to literature by people awake to methodological interest, much spadework has been done. In the work of Lem and the critics from *Science-Fiction Studies* (see Bibliography) we may even possess some cornerstones for a needed critical home. If one may speculate on some fundamental features or indeed axioms of such criticism, the first might be the already mentioned one that the genre has to be evaluated proceeding from its heights down, applying the standards gained by the analysis of its masterpieces. The second axiom might be to demand of SF a level of cognition higher than that of its average reader: the strange novelty is its *raison d'être*. As a minimum, we must demand from SF that it be wiser than the world it speaks to.

In other words, this is an educational literature, hopefully less deadening than most compulsory education in our split national and class societies, but irreversibly shaped by the pathos of preaching the good word of human curiosity, fear, and hope. Significant SF (to which, as in all genres—but somewhat disappointingly so—at least 95 percent of printed matter claiming the name does not belong) denies thus the "two-cultures gap" more efficiently than any other literary genre I know of. Even more importantly, it demands from the author and reader, teacher and critic, not merely specialized, quantified positivistic knowledge (*scientia*) but a social imagination whose quality, whose wisdom (*sapientia*), testifies to the maturity of his critical and creative thought.

The Time-Travel Story and Related
Matters of SF Structuring

by Stanislaw Lem

Let's look at a couple of simple sentences which logic, by virtue of a "disconnected middle" or by virtue of a tautology, asserts are always true, and let's investigate whether there can be worlds in which their veracity ceases. The first will be the ever real disjuncture: "John is the father of Peter or John is not the father of Peter." Any logician would acknowledge that this disjuncture satisfies at all times the requirement for truth since *tertium non datur,* it is impossible to be 40% father and 60% non-father.

Next, let's work with a complex sentence: "If Peter has sexual relations with his mother, then Peter commits incest." The implication is a tautological one since, according to the semantic rules of language, to have sexual relations with one's mother is tantamount to committing incest. (Our conjunction is not a complete tautology since incest constitutes a concept broader than sexual relations with a mother, referring rather to relations with any person of such close kinship. We could bring the sentence to a perfect tautology, but this would necessitate complexities which would in no way alter the essence of the matter and merely make the argumentation more difficult.)

To simplify matters we shall investigate first the impact of changes on the veracity or falsity of the statement "John is the father of Peter." We should point out that what is involved here is a truly causative biological relation to the birth of a child, and not the ambiguous use of the designation "father" (since it is indeed possible to be a biological father and not be a baptismal father, or conversely, to be a godfather, but not a parent).

"The Time-Travel Story and Related Matters of SF Structuring" by Stanislaw Lem, translated from the Polish by Thomas H. Hoisington and Darko Suvin. From *Science Fiction Studies*, I (1974), pp. 143–54. Reprinted by permission of *Science Fiction Studies* and The Seabury Press.

Suppose John is a person who died three hundred years ago, but whose reproductive cells were preserved by refrigeration. A woman fertilized by them will become Peter's mother. Will John then be Peter's father? Undoubtedly.

But then suppose the following: John died and did not leave reproductive cells, but a woman asked a genetic technician to make up in laboratory a spermatozoon of John from a single preserved cell of John's epithelium (all the cells of the body having the same genetic composition). Will John, once fertilization is complete, now also be Peter's father?

Now suppose the following case: John not only died, but did not leave a single bodily cell. Instead, John left a will in which he expressed the desire that a genetic technician perform the steps necessary to enable a woman to become the mother of a child of John, i.e. that such a woman give birth to a child and that the child be markedly similar to John. In addition, the genetic technician is not permitted to use any spermatozoa. Rather, he is supposed to cause a parthenogenetic development of the female ovum. Along with this he is supposed to control the genic substance and direct it by embryogenetic transformations in such a way that the Peter born is "the spit and image of John" (there are photographs of John available, a recording of his voice, etc.). The geneticist "sculptures" in the chromosomal substance of the woman all the features John craved for in a child. And thus, to the question "Is John the father or not the father of Peter?" it is now impossible to give an unequivocal answer of "yes" or "no." In some senses John is indeed the father, but in others he is not. An appeal to empiricism alone will not in itself furnish a clear answer. The definition will be essentially determined by the cultural standards of the society in which John, Peter's mother, Peter, as well as the genetic technician, all live.

Let's assume that these standards are fixed, and that the child realized in strict accordance with John's testamental instructions is generally acknowledged to be his child. If, however, the genetic technician either on his own or at the instigation of others made up 45% of the genotypical features of the child not in accordance with the stipulations of the will, but in accordance with an entirely different prescription, it would then be impossible to maintain that John, in agreement with the standards of a given culture, either is or is not the child's father. The situation is the same as when some experts say about a picture reputed to be a work of Rembrandt: "This is a canvas by Rembrandt" while others say: "This is not a canvas by Rembrandt." Since it is quite possible that Rembrandt began the picture, but that some anonymous person finished the work, then 47% of the work could be said to originate from Rembrandt, and 53% from someone else. In such a situation of "partial authorship," *tertium datur.* In other words, there are situations in which it is possible to be a father only in part. (It is also possible to achieve such situations in other ways, e.g., by removing a certain number of genes from a spermatozoon of John and substituting another person's genes for them.)

The possibilities of the transformations mentioned above, which entail a change in the logical value of the disjunction—"John is the father of Peter or John is not the father of Peter"—lie, one may judge, in the bosom of a not too distant future. Thus a work describing such a matter would be fantastic today, but thirty or fifty years hence it might indeed be realistic. However, the work by no means needs to relate the story of a definite, concrete John, Peter, and mother of Peter. It could describe fictitious persons in a manner typical of any form of literary composition. The relational invariables between father, mother, and child would not have at that time the fictitious nature they have in the present. The invariables that concern paternity are today different from those of a time when genetic engineering would be realized. In this sense a composition written today and depicting a given situation without a "disconnected middle" in the predication of paternity, may be considered a futurological prognosis or a hypothesis which may prove to be true.

For a real tautology to become a falsehood, the device of *travel in time* is necessary. Suppose Peter, having grown up, learns that his father was a very vile person, *viz.* that he seduced Peter's mother and abandoned her only to disappear without a trace. Burning with the desire to bring his father to account for so despicable an act and unable to locate him in the present, Peter boards a time vehicle, sets out for the past and seeks out the father in the vicinity of the place where his mother was supposed to have resided at that time. The search, although very thorough, turns out to be in vain. However, in the course of establishing various contacts related to his expedition, Peter meets a young girl who attracts him. The two fall in love and a baby is conceived. Peter, however, cannot remain permanently in the past; he is obliged to return to his old mother, for whom he is the sole support. Having been convinced by the girl that she has not become pregnant, Peter returns to the present. He has not succeeded in finding traces of his father. One day he finds in one of his mother's drawers a thirty-year-old photograph and to his horror recognizes in it the girl whom he loved. Not wishing to impede him, she committed a white lie, and hid her pregnancy. Peter thus comes to understand that he did not find his father for the simple enough reason that he himself is the father. So, Peter journeyed into the past to search for a missing father, assuming the name of John to facilitate his search by remaining incognito. The upshot of this journey is his own birth. Thus, we have before us a circular causal structure. Peter is his own father, but, as against a superficial judgment, he did not commit incest at all, since, when he had sexual intercourse with her, his mother was not (and could not be) his mother. (From a purely genetic point of view, if we forget that—as is today believed—the causal circle is impossible, Peter is genotypically identical with his mother. In other words, Peter's mother for all practical purposes gave birth to him parthenogenetically since, of course, no man inseminated her who was alien to her.)

This structure constitutes the so-called time loop, a causal structure characteristic of an enormous number of SF compositions. The composition which I described is a "minimal" loop, yet there is one still "smaller," created by Robert Heinlein in the story "All You Zombies" (1959). Its plot is as follows: a certain young girl becomes pregnant by a man who then promptly disappears. She bears a child, or more correctly, gives birth to it by Caesarean section. During the operation, the doctors ascertain that she is a hermaphrodite and it is essential (for reasons not explained by the author) to change her sex. She leaves the clinic as a young man who, because he was until quite recently a woman, has given birth to a child. She seeks her seducer for a long time, until it comes to light that *she herself* is he. We have the following circular situation: one and the same individual was in time T1 both a girl and her partner since the girl, transformed into a man by surgical intervention, was transferred by the narrator to time T1 from a future time,

T2. The narrator, a time traveller, "removed" the young man from time T2 and transferred him to time T1 so that the latter seduced "himself."

Nine months after time T1 the child was born. The narrator stole this child and took it back in time twenty years, to moment T0, so he could leave it under the trees of a foundling home. So the circle is completely closed: the same individual comprises "father," "mother," and "child." In other words, a person impregnated himself and gave birth to himself. The baby, born as a result of this, is left behind in time, bringing about in twenty years the growth of a girl who has in time T1 sex with a young man from time T2. The young man is she herself, transformed into a man by a surgical operation. The fact that a sexual hermaphrodite should not be able to bear a child is a relatively small hindrance, since the puzzling situation of a person's giving birth to himself is considerably "more impossible." What we are dealing with here is an act of *creatio ex nihilo*. All structures of the time loop variety are internally contradictory in a causal sense. The contradictoriness, however, is not always as apparent as in Heinlein's story.

Frederic Brown writes about a man who travels into the past in order to punish his grandfather for tormenting his grandmother. In the course of an altercation he kills his grandfather before his father has been engendered. Thus the time traveller cannot then come into the world. Who, therefore, in fact killed the grandfather, if the murderer has not come into the world at all? Herein lies the contradiction. Sometimes an absent-minded scientist, having left something in the past which he has visited, returns for the lost object and encounters his own self, since he has not returned exactly to the moment after his departure for the present, but to the time-point at which he was before. When such returns are repeated, the individual is subject to multiple reproduction in the form of doubles. Since such possibilities appear to be pointless, in one of my stories about Ion Tichy (the "7th Journey"), I maximalized "duplication" of the central character. Ion Tichy's spaceship finds itself in gravitational whirlpools that bend time into a circle, so that the space-ship is filled with a great number of different Ions.

The loop motif can be used, for instance, in the following ways: someone proceeds into the past, deposits ducats in a Venetian bank at compound interest, and centuries later in New York demands from a consortium of banks payment of the entire capital, a gigantic sum. Why does he need so much money all of a sudden? So that he can hire the best physicists to construct for him a thus far nonexistent time vehicle, and by means of this vehicle go back in time to Venice where he will deposit ducats at compound interest ... (Mack Reynolds, "Compounded Interest" [1956]). Or another example: in the future someone comes to an artist (in one story to a painter, in another to a writer) and gives him either a book dealing with painting in the future or a novel written in the future. The artist then begins to imitate this material as much as possible, and becomes famous, the paradox being that he is borrowing from his own self (since he himself was the author of that book or those pictures, only "twenty years later").

We learn, further, from various works of this sort how the Mesozoic reptiles became extinct thanks to hunters who organized a "safari into the past" (Frederic Brown), or how, in order to move in time in one direction, an equal mass must be displaced in the opposite direction, or how expeditions in time can reshape historical events. The latter theme has been used time and again, as in one American tale in which the Confederate States are victorious over the North (Ward Moore's *Bring the Jubilee* [1952/1953]). The hero, a military historian, sets out for the past in order to investigate how the Southerners gained victory near Gettysburg. His arrival in a time machine, however, throws General Lee's troop formations into disarray, which results in victory for the North. The hero is no longer able to return to the future, because his arrival also disturbed the causal chain upon which the subsequent construction of his time machine depended. Thus, the person who was supposed to have financed the construction of the machine will not do this, the machine will not exist, and the historian will be stuck in the year 1863 without the means to travel back into the original time. Of course here also there is an inherent paradox—just how did he reach the past? As a rule, the fun consists in the way the paradox is shifted from one segment of the action to another. The time loop as the backbone of a work's causal structure is thus different from the far looser motif of journeys in time per se; but, of course, it is merely a logical, although extreme, consequence of the general acceptance of the possibility of "chronomotion." There are actually two possible authorial attitudes which are mutually exclusive: either one deliberately demonstrates causal paradoxes resulting from "chronomotion" with the greatest possible consistency, or else one cleverly avoids them. In the first instance, the careful development of logical consequences leads to situations as absurd as the one cited (an individual that is his very own father, that procreates himself), and usually has a comic effect (though this does not follow automatically).

Even though a circular causal structure may signalize a frivolous type of content, this does not mean that it is necessarily reduced to the construction of comic antinomies for the sake of pure entertainment. The causal circle may be employed not as the goal of the story, but as a means of visualizing certain theses, e.g. from the philosophy of history. Slonimski's story of the Time Torpedo belongs here. It is a belletristic assertion of the "*ergo*ness" or ergodicity of history: monkeying with events which have had sad consequences does not bring about any improvement of history; instead of one group of disasters and wars there simply comes about another, in no way better set.

A diametrically opposed hypothesis, on the other hand, is incorporated into Ray Bradbury's "A Sound of Thunder" (1952). In an excellently written short episode, a participant in a "safari for tyrannosaurs" tramples a butterfly and a couple of flowers, and by that microscopic act causes such perturbances of causal chains involving millions of years, that upon his return the English language has a different orthography and a different candidate—not liberal but rather a kind of dictator—has won in the presidential election. It is only a pity that Bradbury feels obliged to set in motion complicated and unconvincing explanations to account for the fact that hunting for reptiles, which indeed fall from shots, disturbs nothing in the causal chains, whereas the trampling of a tiny flower does (when a tyrannosaur drops to the ground, the quantity of ruined flowers must be greater than when the safari participant descends from a safety zone to the ground). "A Sound of Thunder" exemplifies an "anti-ergodic" hypothesis of history, as opposed to Slonimski's story. In a way, however, the two are reconcilable: History can as a whole be "ergodic" if not very responsive to local disturbances, and at the same time such exceptional hypersensitive points in the causal chains can exist, the vehement disturbance of which produces more intensive results. In personal affairs such a "hyperallergic point" would be, for example, a situation in which a car attempts to pass a truck at the same time that a second car is approaching from the opposite direction.

As is usually the case in SF, a theme defined by a certain devised structure of occurrences (in this instance pertaining to a journey in time) undergoes a characteristic cognitive-artistic involution. We could have demonstrated this for any given theme, but let's take advantage of the opportunity at hand.

At first, authors and readers are satisfied by the joy of discerning the effects of innovations still virginal as far as their inherent contradictions are concerned. Then, an intense search is begun for initial situations which allow for the most effective exploitation of consequences that are potentially present in a given structure. Thus, the devices of chronomotion begin supporting, e.g., theses of history and philosophy (concerned with the "ergodicity" or non-ergodicity of history). Then, grotesque and humorous stories like Frederic Brown's "The Yehudi Principle" (1944) appear: this short story is *itself* a causal circle (it ends with the words that it began with: it describes a test of a device for fulfilling wishes; one of the wishes expressed is that a story "write itself," which is what just happened).

Finally, the premise of time travel serves frequently as a simple pretext for weaving tales of sensational, criminal, or melodramatic intrigue; this usually involves the revival and slight refurbishment of petrified plots.

Time travel has been used so extensively in SF that it has been divided into separate sub-categories. There is, e.g., the category of *missent parcels* that find their way into the present from the future: someone receives a "Build-a-Man Set" box with "freeze-dried nerve preparations," bones, etc.; he builds his own double, and an "inspector from the future," who comes to reclaim the parcel, disassembles instead of the artificial twin, the very hero of the story; this is William Tenn's "Child's Play" (1947). In Damon Knight's "Thing of Beauty" (1958) there is a different parcel—an automaton that draws pictures by itself. In general, strange things are produced in the future, SF teaches us (e.g., polka-dotted paint as well as thousands of objects with secret names and purposes not known).

Another category is *tiers in time*. In its simplest form it is presented in Anthony Boucher's "The Barrier" (1942), a slightly satiric work. The hero, travelling to the future, comes to a state of "eternal stasis," which, to protect its perfect stagnation from all disturbances, has constructed "time barriers" that foil any penetration. Now and then, however, a barrier becomes pervious. Rather disagreeable conditions prevail in this state which is ruled by a police similar to the Gestapo (Stapper). One must be a slightly more advanced SF reader to follow the story. The hero finds his way immediately into a circle of people who know him very well, but whom he does not know at all. This is explained by the fact that in order to elude the police he goes somewhat further back in time. He at that time gets to know these very people, then considerably younger. He is for them a stranger, but he, while he was in the future, has already succeeded in getting to know them. An old lady, who got into the time vehicle with the hero when they were fleeing from the police, meets as a result her own self as a young person and suffers a severe shock. It is clear, however, that Boucher does not know what to do with the "encountering oneself" motif in this context, and therefore makes the lady's shock long and drawn out. Further jumps in time, one after another, complicate the intrigue in a purely formal way. Attempts are begun to overthrow the dictatorial government, but everything goes to pieces, providing in the process sensationalism. *Anti-problematic escapism into adventure* is a very common phenomenon in SF: authors indicate its formal effectiveness, understood as the ingenious setting of a game in motion, as the skill of achieving uncommon *movements*, without mastering and utilizing the problematic and semantic aspects of such kinematics.

Such authors neither discuss nor solve the problems raised by their writing, but rather "take care" of them by dodges, employing patterns like the happy ending or the setting in motion of sheer pandemonium, a chaos which quickly engulfs loose meanings.

Such a state of affairs is a result of the distinctly "ludic" or playful position of writers; they go for an effect as a tank goes for an obstacle: without regard for anything incidental. It is as if their field of vision were greatly intensified and, simultaneously, also greatly confined. As in Tenn's story, the consequences of a "temporal lapse" in a postal matter are everything. Let us call such a vision *monoparametric.* At issue is a situation which is bizarre, amusing, uncanny, logically developed from a structural premise (e.g., from the presupposition of "journeys in time," which implies a qualitative difference in the world's causal structure). At the same time such a vision does not deal with anything more than that.

This can be seen readily from an example of "maximal intensification" of the subject of *governments in time* or "chronocracy," described by Isaac Asimov in his novel *The End of Eternity* (1955). "The Barrier" showed a single state isolating itself in the historical flow of events, as once the Chinese attempted to isolate themselves from the disturbing influences by building the Chinese wall (a spatially exact equivalent of a "time barrier"). *The End of Eternity* shows a government in power throughout humanity's entire temporal existence. Inspector-generals, travelling in time, examine the goings on in individual epochs, centuries, and millenia, and by calculating the probability of occurrences and then counteracting the undesirable ones, keep in hand the entire system—"history extended in a four-dimensional continuum"—in a state of desirable equilibrium. Obviously, presuppositions of this sort are more thickly larded with antinomies than is the scrawniest hare larded with bacon. While Asimov's great proficiency is manifested by the size of the slalom over which the narrative runs, it is, in the end, an ineffably naive conception because no issues from philosophy or history are involved. The problem of "closed millenia," which the "tempocrats" do not have access to, is explained when a certain beautiful girl, whom an inspector falls in love with, turns out to be not a lowly inhabitant of one of the centuries under the dominion of the tempocracy, but a secret emissary from the "inaccessible millenia." The time dictatorship as a control over the continuum of history will be destroyed, and a liberated humanity will be able to take up astronautics and other select suitable occupations. The enigma of the inaccessible millenia is remarkably similar to the "enigma of the closed room" found in fairy tales and detective stories. The various epochs about which the emissaries of the chronocracy hover also recall separate rooms. *The End of Eternity* is an exhibition of formal entertainment to which sentiments about the fight for freedom and against dictatorship have been tacked on rather casually.

We have already spoken about the "minimal time loop." Let us talk now, simply for the sake of symmetry, about the "maximal" loops.

A. E. van Vogt has approached this concept in *The Weapon Shops of Isher* (1949/1951), but let's expound it in our own way. As is known, there is a hypothesis (it can be found in Feynman's physics) which states that positrons are electrons moving "against the tide" in the flow of time. It is also known that in principle, even galaxies can arise from atomic collisions, as long as the colliding atoms are sufficiently rich in energy. In accordance with these presuppositions we can construct the following story: in a rather distant future a celebrated cosmologist reaches, on the basis of his own research as well as that of all his predecessors, the irrefutable conclusion that, on the one hand, the cosmos came into being from a single particle and, on the other, that such a single particle could not have existed—where could it have sprung from? Thus he is confronted with a dilemma: the cosmos has come into being, but it could not come into being! He is horrified by this revelation, but, after profound reflections, suddenly sees the light: the cosmos exists exactly as mesons sometimes exist; mesons, admittedly, break the law of conservation, but do this so quickly that they do not break it. The cosmos exists on credit! It is like a debenture, a draft for material and energy which *must* be repaid immediately, because its existence is the purest one hundred percent liability both in terms of energy and in terms of material. Then, just what does the cosmologist do? With the help of physicist friends he builds a great "chronogun" which fires one single electron backward "against the tide" in the flow of time. That electron, transformed into a positron as a result of its motion "against the grain" of time, goes speeding through time, and in the course of this journey acquires more and more energy. Finally, at the point where it "leaps out" of the cosmos, i.e. in a place in which there had *as yet* been no cosmos, all the terrible energies it has acquired are released in that tremendously powerful explosion which brings about the Universe! In this manner the debt is paid off. At the same time, thanks to the largest possible "causal circle," the existence of the cosmos is authenticated, and a person turns out to be the actual creator of that very Universe! It is possible to complicate this story slightly, for example, by telling how certain colleagues of the cosmologist, unpleasant and envious people, meddled in his work, shooting on their own some lesser particles backwards against the tide of time. These particles exploded inaccurately when the cosmologist's positron was producing the cosmos, and because of this that unpleasant rash came into being which bothers science so much today, namely the enigmatic quasars and pulsars which are not readily incorporated into the corpus of contemporary knowledge. These then are the "artifacts" produced by the cosmologist's malicious competitors. It would also be possible to tell how humanity both created and depraved itself, because some physicist shot the "chronogun" hurriedly and carelessly and a particle went astray, exploding as a nova in the vicinity of the solar system two million years ago, and damaging by its hard radiance the hereditary plasma of the original anthropoids who therefore did not evolve into "man good and rational" as "should have happened" without the new particle. In other words, the new particle caused the degeneration of Homo sapiens—witness his history.

In this version, then, we created the cosmos only in a mediocre fashion, and our own selves quite poorly. Obviously a work of this sort, in whichever variant, becomes ironical, independently of its basic notion (i.e. the "self-creative" application of the "maximal time loop").

As one can see, what is involved is an intellectual game, actually fantasy-making which alters in a logical or pseudo-logical manner current scientific hypotheses. This is "pure" Science-Fiction, or Science-Fantasy as it is sometimes called. It shows us nothing serious, but merely demonstrates the consequences of a reasoning which, operating within the guidelines of the scientific method, is used sometimes in unaltered form (in predicting the "composition percentage of paternity" we have in no way altered the scientific data), and sometimes secretly modified. And thus SF can be responsibly or irresponsibly plugged into the hypothesis-creating system of scientific thought.

The example of "self-creation" reveals first of all the "maximal proportions" of a self-perpetrating paradox: Peter gave birth only to himself, whereas in the universal variant, mankind concocted itself, and, what is more, perhaps not in the best manner, so that it would be even possible to use "Manichaean" terminology. Furthermore, this example at the same time demonstrates that the

conceptual premise of essential innovations in the structure of the
objective world presented is central to a science-fictional work (in
the case of journeys in time, a change in causality is involved, by
admitting the reversibility of that which we consider today as
universally and commonly irreversible). The qualities of fictional
material which serve a dominant concept are thus subject to an
assessment based on the usefulness to this concept. Fictional
material should in that case be an embodiment of a pseudo-
scholarly or simply scholarly hypothesis—and that's all. Thus
"pure" SF arises, appealing exclusively to "pure reason." It is
possible to complicate a work with problems lying beyond the scope
of such an intellectual game: when, e.g., the "Manichaeism of
existence" is interpreted as due to an error of an envious physicist,
then an opportunity for sarcasm or irony arises as a harmonic
"overtone" above the narrative's main axis. But by doing this, we
have forced SF to perform "impure" services, because it is then not
delivering scientific pseudo-revelations, but functioning in the same
semantic substratum in which literature has normally operated. It
is because of this that we call SF contaminated by semantic
problems *"relational* SF."

However, just as "normal" literature can also perform high and
low services—produce sentimental love stories and epics—*relational*
SF shows an analogous amplitude. As was noted, it is possible to
interpret it allegorically (e.g., Manichaeism in relation to the
creation of the cosmos)—and this will be the direction of grotesque
or humorous departures from a state of "intellectual purity" which
is somewhat analogous to "mathematical vacuity." It is also
possible to overlay the history of creating the cosmos with melodrama, e.g., to make it part of a sensational, psychopathological
intrigue (the cosmologist who created the Universe has a wicked
wife whom he nonetheless loves madly; or, the cosmologist becomes
possessed; or also, faced with his deeds, the cosmologist goes insane
and, as a megalomaniac, will be treated slightingly in an insane
asylum, etc.).

Thus, in the end, the realistic writer is not responsible for the
overall—e.g., the causal—structure of the real world. In evaluating
his works, we are not centrally concerned with assessing the
structure of the world to which they nonetheless have some relation.

On the contrary, the SF writer is responsible both for the world in which he has placed his action, and for the action as well, inasmuch as he, within certain limits, invents both one and the other.

However, the invention of new worlds in SF is as rare as a pearl the size of a bread loaf. And so 99.9% of all SF works follow compositionally a scheme, one of the thematic structures which constitute the whole SF repertoire. For a world truly new in structural qualities is one in which the causal irreversibility of occurrences is denied, or one in which a person's individuality conflicts with an individual scientifically produced by means of an "intellectronic evolution," or one in which Earthly culture is in communication with a non-Earthly culture distinct from human culture not only nominally but *qualitatively*, and so forth. However, just as it is impossible to invent a steam engine, or an internal combustion engine, or any other already existing thing, it is also impossible to invent once more worlds with the sensational quality of "chronomotion" or of "a reasoning machine." As the detective story churns out unweariedly the same plot stereotypes, so does SF when it tells us of countless peripeties merely to show that by interposing a time loop they have been successfully invalidated (e.g. in Thomas Wilson's "The Entrepreneur" [1952] which talks about the dreadful Communists having conquered the USA, and time travellers who start backwards at the necessary point, invalidating such an invasion and dictatorship). In lieu of Communists, there may be Aliens or even the Same People Arriving from the Future (thanks to the time loop, anyone can battle with himself just as long as he pleases), etc.

If new concepts, those atomic kernels that initiate a whole flood of works, correspond to that gigantic device by which bioevolution was "invented"—i.e., to the constitutional principle of types of animals such as vertebrates and nonvertebrates, or fish, amphibians, mammals, and birds—then, in the "evolution of SF," the equivalent of type-creating revolutions were the ideas of *time travel*, of *constructing a robot*, of *cosmic contact*, of *cosmic invasion*, and of *ultimate catastrophe for the human species*. And, as within the organization of biological types a natural evolution imperceptibly produces distinctive changes according to genera, families, races, and so forth—similarly, SF persistently operates within a framework of modest, simply variational craftsmanship.

This very craftsmanship, however, betrays a systematic, unidirectional bias: as we stated and demonstrated, great concepts that alter the structure of the fictional world are a manifestation of a pure play of the intellect. The results are assessed according to the type of play. The play can also be "relational," involved with situations only loosely or not at all connected with the dominant principle. What connection is there, after all, between the existence of the cosmologist who created the world, and the fact that he has a beautiful secretary whom he beds? Or, by what if not by a retardation device will the cosmologist be snatched away before he fires the "chronogun"? In this manner an idea lending itself to articulation in a couple of sentences (as we have done here) becomes a pretext for writing a long novel (where a "cosmos-creating" shot comes only in the epilogue, after some deliverers sent by the author have finally saved the cosmologist from his sorry plight). The purely intellectual concept is stretched thoroughly out of proportion to its inherent possibilities. But this is just how SF proceeds—usually.

On the other hand, rarely is a departure made from "emptiness" or "pure play" in the direction of dealing with a set of important and involved problems. For in the world of SF it is structurally as possible to set up an adventure plot as a psychological drama; it is as possible to deal in sensational happenings as it is to stimulate thought by an ontological implication created by the narrative as a whole. It is precisely this slide toward easy, sensational intrigue which is a symptom of the degeneration of this branch of literature. An idea is permitted in SF if it is packaged so that one can barely see it through the glitter of the wrapping. As against conventions only superficially associated to innovations in the world's structure and which have worn completely threadbare from countless repetitions, SF should be stimulated and induced to deviate from this trend of development, namely, by involution away from the "sensational pole." SF should not operate by increasing the number of blasters or Martians who impede the cosmologist in his efforts to fire from the "chronogun"; such inflation is not appropriate. Rather, one should change direction radically and head for the opposite pole. After all, in principle the same bipolar opposition also prevails in ordinary literature, which also shuttles between cheap melodrama and stories with the highest aesthetic and cognitive aspirations.

It is difficult, however, to detect in SF a convalescence or outright salvation of this sort. An odd fate seems to loom heavily over its domain, which prompts writers with the highest ambitions and considerable talent, such as Ray Bradbury or J. G. Ballard, to employ the conceptual and rational tools of SF in an at times admittedly superb way, yet not in order to ennoble the genre, but instead to bring it toward an "optimal" pole of literature. Aiming in that direction, they are simultaneously, in each successive step, giving up the programmatic rationalism of SF in favour of the irrational; their intellect fails to match their know-how and their artistic talent. In practice, what this amounts to is that they do not use the "signalling equipment" of SF, its available accessories, to express any truly, intellectually new problems or content. They try to bring about the conversion of SF to the "creed of normal literature" through articulating, by fantastic means, such non-fantastic content which is already old-fashioned in an ethical, axiological, philosophical sense. The revolt against the machine and against civilization, the praise of the "aesthetic" nature of catastrophe, the dead-end course of human civilization—these are their foremost problems, the intellectual content of their works. Such SF is as it were a priori vitiated by pessimism, in the sense that anything that may happen will be for the worse.

Such writers proceed as if they thought that, should mankind acknowledge the existence of even a one-in-a-million or one-in-a-billion chance—transcending the already known cyclical pulsation of history, which has oscillated between a state of relative stabilization and of complete material devastation—such an approach would not be proper. Only in mankind's severe, resolute rejection of all chances of development, in complete negation, in a gesture of escapism or nihilism, do they find the proper mission of all SF which would not be cheap. Consequently they build on dead-end tragedy. This may be called into question not merely from the standpoint of optimism, of whatever hue and intensity. Rather, one should criticize their ideology by attempting to prove that they tear to shreds that which they themselves do not understand. With regard to the formidable movements which shake our world, they nourish the same fear of *misunderstanding* the mechanisms of change that every ordinary form of literature has. Isn't it clear what proportions their defection assumes because of this? *Cognitive* optimism is, first of all, a thoroughly non-ludic premise in the creation of SF. The result is often extremely cheap, artistically as well as intellectually, but its principle is good. According to this principle, there is only one remedy for imperfect knowledge: better knowledge, because more varied knowledge. SF, to be sure, normally supplies numerous surrogates for such knowledge. But, according to its premises, that knowledge exists and is accessible: the irrationalism of Bradbury's or Ballard's fantasy negates both these premises. One is not allowed to entertain any cognitive hopes—that becomes the unwritten axiom of their work. Instead of introducing into traditional qualities of writing new conceptual equipment as well as new notional configurations relying on intellectual imagination, these authors, while ridding themselves of the stigma of cheap and defective SF, in one fell swoop give up all that constitutes its cognitive value. Obviously, they are unaware of the consequences of such desertion, but this only clears them morally: so much the worse for literature and for culture, seriously damaged by their mistake.

Genre Criticism:
Science Fiction and the Fantastic

by Eric S. Rabkin

Genre criticism is criticism of works of art distributed into classes. In the study of art, *genre* means *class.* In literature, classes are defined in diverse ways, many inconsistent with each other. For example, one might wish to study the genre of *Elizabethan tragedies*; that is, works written in English, during the reign of Elizabeth I, intended for stage performance, and having something to do with the fall of great personages. Elizabeth died in 1603; *King Lear* was written in 1606. But still *King Lear* is Elizabethan, if not in date, then in mood and surely a matter of three years shouldn't prevent a work from being considered in its proper context. Propriety here reflects the perspectives of the reader, of the observer for whom selecting works along certain lines seems interesting and profitable. One could as well define a genre only by the number of verse lines, like the *sonnet;* or define a *genre* by its political content, like *Marxist literature.* The choice of a genre definition, a choice habitually made both conventionally and unconsciously, is a choice that reflects the perspectives of the reader. When we recommend one book to a friend as being "like" another, the grounds for similarity can be almost anything, so long as they include those elements of the work that we believe have made the first book valuable to our friend. Such a recommendation is an act of genre criticism.

The wide range of works which we have already seen fit to call, in one degree or another, fantastic, is large, much too large to constitute a single genre. We have embraced whole conventional genres, such as *fairy tale, detective story,* and *fantasy*[1], and we have seen that as genres they may be related according to the degree and kind of their use of the fantastic. For this very reason, study of those elements that make a work fantastic gives us a new vantage on works previously classed only according to established generic divisions. ...

The term *science fiction* has been forced into many different kinds of service. Although coined by Hugo Gernsback in 1926 to denote the all-male technological adventure stories which he was writing and editing, the term has since been made to include the voyage to Laputa in *Gulliver's Travels* (1726) and the *Icaromenippus* of Lucian of Samosota (b. 120 A.D.); it includes "Sword and Sorcery" novels like *A Private Cosmos* by Philip José Farmer and rigorously logical tales like the robotics stories of Isaac Asimov; it includes the sweetly lyrical romanticism of Ray Bradbury in *The Martian Chronicles* and the unashamed machismo militarism of Robert A. Heinlein in *Starship Troopers*; it includes novels of warning and prediction like Nevil Shute's *On the Beach* and such historic impossibilities as novels of alternate time-streams like Moorcock's *Warlord of the Air*; it includes such enthusiastically technological tales as the "Star Trek"

---

[1] The only theoretical work specifically on *fantasy* is Tzvetan Todorov, *The Fantastic: A Structural Approach To A Literary Genre*, Richard Howard, transl., Case Western Reserve University Press, 1973 (1970). This is a book with many excellences which, in numerous ways, complements the current study. However, in many regards, these two works are in serious disagreement. An exhaustive comparison would needlessly sidetrack this inquiry, but two points may be worth making. First, Todorov radically limits not only Fantasy, but the fantastic, to the realm of a single genre. "Not all fictions ... are linked to the fantastic," (p. 75) he writes, even though he recognizes that the fantastic is generated by "as if," which I would see, with Worringer, as inherent in all art. Second, Todorov locates the affect of the fantastic in "the reader's hesitation" (p. 32) in determining whether a narrated event must be taken as merely metaphoric (moving the text into a genre he calls the *marvelous*) or actual (moving the text into a genre he calls the *uncanny*). "The fantastic occupies the duration of this uncertainty." (p. 25) This is an acute and useful insight; however, it must be modified in two ways to capitalize on it. First, this hesitation should be seen not in relation to external norms, but rather in relation to microcontextual variations; second, one must realize that keeping track of this affect, and locating it in other aspects of narrative than plot, can give us an organizing principle for studies larger than those of Todorov's "literary genre." His is a thoughtful, suggestive, and useful book—one that anticipates some of the work here, but it is a book which ultimately reflects a different view of the fantastic.

series begun by James Blish and such a-technological tales as *A Canticle for Leibowitz*, Walter M. Miller, Jr.'s exploration of institutional stability and historical periodicity. And there are other works by these and other authors that slip in and out of the genre with hardly anyone noticing.

One definition that seems to encompass the diverse works we have mentioned is this: a work belongs in the genre of *science fiction* if its narrative world is at least somewhat different from our own, and if that difference is apparent against the background of an organized body of knowledge. Some qualifications may make this definition clearer.

As with the fantastic, the notion of difference, though generally definable in relation to "our" world, actually must be defined in terms of the world outside the text as that text recreates it. Although today we have speedy and deadly submarines, *20,000 Leagues Under the Sea* (1869) is still science fiction for two reasons: first, Professor Aronnax makes clear that the science of Verne's day would never expect ships to be sunk by submarine ("... the theory of an underwater *Monitor* was definitively rejected ..." [2]) and second, the grapholect of the text recalls the pre-submarine era. *Difference* then, in defining *science fiction,* refers to a microcontextual variation. When this variation is a full 180-degree reversal of a ground rule (for example, in a quantum-mechanics-dominated tale, the action might suddenly depend on the anti-expected phenomenon of speeds faster than that of light) then the science fiction tale is fantastic. If the variation is merely a use of the disexpected (for example, intelligent life that reproduces by fission), then the tale is much less fantastic. The variation from accepted knowledge is one of the defining characteristics of the genre of science fiction, and it is a characteristic that we can use to carefully subdivide the genre for purposes of analysis.

A second qualification to our definition concerns the notion of *organized body of knowledge.* The term *science* calls hardware to mind, but much science fiction really makes only subordinate use of technology. The real "science" behind Ursula K. LeGuin's study of the social importance of sex as a role indicator (*The Left Hand of*

[2] Jules Verne, *20,000 Leagues Under the Sea*, Anthony Bonner, transl., Bantam, New York, 1962 (1869), p. 20.

Darkness, 1969) is anthropology, not physics or chemistry or even biology. In *Pavane* (1966) by Keith Roberts, we have a world set in the mid-1960s, but it concerns the history of a world that shared our history until 1588, at which point the Spanish fleet *conquered* the English. The consistency of Roberts' alternative world depends on extrapolations of the laws of history, economic determinism, scientific evolution. What is important in the definition of science fiction is not the appurtenances of ray guns and lab coats, but the "scientific" habits of mind: the idea that paradigms do control our view of all phenomena, that within these paradigms all normal problems can be solved, and that abnormal occurrences must either be explained or initiate the search for a better (usually more inclusive) paradigm. In science fiction, these habits of mind and their associated bodies of knowledge determine the outcome of events, regardless of which science most obviously informs the narrative world. In that regard, like the puzzle tales of detective fiction, all science fiction is to some extent fantastic.

A special case of this definition by *difference* and *organized body of knowledge* is the prescription that a good work of science fiction make one and only one assumption about its narrative world which violates that which is known about our own world and then extrapolate the whole narrative world from that difference. In letting the Spanish armada win, *Pavane* satisfies this reduced definition (though many other works, like *A Voyage to Arcturus*, do not). This truncated prescription has great heuristic power. Modern science fiction developed most strongly in the United States and then England. For both these communities, the primary antecedent was H. G. Wells, and Wells followed this prescription instinctively. In *The Time Machine* (1895), for example, we are told in italics: *"There is no difference between Time and any of the three dimensions of Space except that our consciousness moves along it."* [3] Granted this fantastic assumption, Wells proceeded to journey to his famous future in which industrialism has made the leisure class into effete and useless children (Eloi) and the working class into loveless and ruthless monsters (Morlocks). Wells had studied (1884–1887) with evolutionist T. H. Huxley and was to be one of the most distinguished members (1903–1908) of the socialist Fabian Society. *The Time*

[3] H. G. Wells, *The Time Machine*, Berkley Highland, New York, 1963 (1895), p. 7.

Machine uses the fantastic idea of time travel (a reversal of the perspectives of classical mechanics) to present a vivid social warning based on orthodox extrapolations of the biology and political science current at the end of the century.

Understanding that the field is broader than the prescriptive definition we can use to locate the works of Wells, we can still take *The Time Machine* as a paradigmatic work of science fiction. Another work which satisfies even the Wellsian purist definition of science fiction is Theodore Sturgeon's *More Than Human* (1953), a novel of the emergence of man's superior future. A comparison of this work with Arthur C. Clarke's *Childhood's End* (1953) will show one of the ways by which consideration of the fantastic can complement normal genre criticism.

More Than Human is a very well-written work. In the year following its publication, it was awarded the International Fantasy Award by a panel of critics selected at the British (science fiction) convention. In this novel, we read of the emergence of *"Homo Gestalt,* the next step upward ... why not a psychic evolution instead of the physical?"[4] This is the assumption we need to grant. The Gestalt creature we are primarily concerned with is a co-ordinated telepathic entity made up of two teleports (Beanie and Bonnie, the apparently idiotic twin offspring of a janitor), a telekine (Janie, who can make objects move through space, or non-space, at will), a computational super-brain (Baby, a nonverbal, nongrowing grotesque change-of-life baby who communicates by direct telepathy with Janie and through her with the nonsenders Beanie and Bonnie), and a Head. The story proceeds as pure science fiction if we grant that people, especially emotional people, and especially children, have potential psychic powers if only these are not obscured by education; that is, if these powers are not repressed by social training and its primary tool, verbal communication.

The book opens with Lone, an adult idiot who is sensitive to the telepathic signals of children because he is a wild creature himself, having escaped an orphanage and having somehow learned to survive in the woods. Janie is introduced next, a child whose enormous hate keeps her telekinetic powers useable (for instance,

[4] Theodore Sturgeon, *More Than Human*, Ballantine, New York, 1971 (1953), p. 177.

she thinks an ashtray at one of her mother's lovers and floors him). By great good chance, Beanie and Bonnie's father is the janitor in the building in which Janie lives. The teleports and the telekine communicate telepathically, become friends and run away together.

By great good luck again, these wandering children somehow appeal emotionally to Lone's idiotic telepathic receptors. He takes them in and they begin to function together. Later Lone takes in the freakish and abandoned Baby, who becomes the brain of *Homo Gestalt*. Janie, the only full telepath and therefore the communication center of the group, plugs Baby into the nonverbal network and she reports that "Baby was matching every fact she fed him with every other fact that he had been fed previously" (p. 57). *Homo Gestalt* begins to function.

The vocabulary of *teleports* and *telekines*, the computational abilities of Baby, and the careful reporting of the coincidences that slowly went into the accumulation of *Homo Gestalt* imply the perspectives of normal mid-twentieth-century science. However, one question nags the reader: what is the value of an apparently scientific explanation if the odds against any one of these occurrences (the mere existence of teleports, for example) seems astronomical; how much less scientific the explanation seems when one considers the multiplied odds against Janie living in the right apartment building, meeting Lone, and so on. This question of coincidence seems to undercut the novel as an example of pure Wellsian science fiction.

In the second part of the novel, we concentrate on Gerry Thompson, a hating young man who finally comes to be the new, and much improved, Head when Lone dies. Gerry alone can kill a man or absorb his memory by mere eye contact; he can force someone to do his will. With Gerry as Head, *Homo Gestalt* has multiplied power, and Gerry's will is now informed by the capabilities of the group entity. *Homo Gestalt* is a potentially terrible beast, but a terrible beast with nothing much to do. Money is easy, and then what? Janie refuses to cooperate when Gerry decides to exercise their collective power for evil and together they have no corporate vision for good.

In the last part of the book, Janie on her own rehabilitates Hip Barrows, whose mind years earlier had been nearly destroyed by

Gerry. Hip is, once reconstructed, very bright, but *not* psychic in any way. Still, he is convinced that he must revenge himself against Gerry. However, when the showdown comes, and Hip has a knife at Gerry's throat, he drops the knife in order to give Gerry a moral education. The shock of kindness is so strong that Gerry pauses to read Hip's mind and motives. Gerry thus learns shame and the scales fall from his eyes. Hip, the nonpsychic, is suddenly revealed as a necessary part of *Homo Gestalt*, "the still small voice" (p. 186) without which the new being cannot properly exist. With Hip plugged in through Janie, and Gerry chastened by Hip, *Homo Gestalt* can begin to function. It's an appealing idea, appealing especially because Sturgeon has created it in such a way that someone like the reader, rather than a telepath, is the keystone of this glorious evolution. A place is made for us. But then, this place can exist only if the other improbable five exist and, against fantastic odds, find each other. The unlikelihood of this seems to make the book illogical; seems to make the book fail as an escape; and seems to prevent the book from actually fulfilling the requirements of its genre.

As soon as Hip has become integrated into *Homo Gestalt*, however, the narrative changes tone as new awarenesses flood upon Gerry and the other members of his Gestalt:

> For a long time the only sound was Gerry's difficult breathing. Suddenly even this stopped, as something happened, something— spoke.
> It came again.
> *Welcome.*
> The voice was a silent one. And here, another, silent too, but another for all that. *It's a new one. Welcome, child!*
> Still another: *Well, well, well! We thought you'd never make it ...*
> Gerry clapped his hands to his mouth. His eyes bulged. Through his mind came a hush of welcoming music. There was warmth and laughter and wisdom. (p. 186)

Gerry's Gestalt has been accepted by the community of Gestalts. We suddenly realize that the coincidences had not been far-fetched at all. The assertion that there are other *Homo Gestalts* implies that telepaths do exist, but we just don't know about them. Our knowledge has been limited by Gerry's, and his had been limited by the other Gestalts. Gerry's Gestalt had thought that it was alone in the world, but only because the other *Homo Gestalts* who had come together earlier for the good of humanity had "quarantined" it. Once made complete by the addition of "the still small voice," Gerry's Gestalt can learn, and we can too, that such Gestalts have been forming, indeed, *guiding* the formation of other Gestalts, all along. By a single stroke, Sturgeon explains logically the one remaining doubt that mars the organic integrity of the book as a work of science fiction. With causation explained precisely on the grounds that we have accepted all along as the *single* allowable deviation from known phenomena, the book achieves unity. This emergent unity seems to justify the immediately following notion that in these *Homo Gestalts* "at last was power which could not corrupt" (p. 188). Since the parts are replaceable, the entity is immortal, and therefore *Homo Gestalt* is, in fact, angelic. Man, with us included as the Hip Barrowses of the world, is shown a vision of heaven. The last line of the book refers to Gerry no longer the vengeful telepath but Gerry the *Homo Gestalt*: "And humbly, he joined their company" (p. 188).

Childhood's End, published in the same year as *More Than Human*, has a great deal in common with it. Although it won no award in its time, readers of Clarke will assert that his book is as well written as Sturgeon's. In fact, *Childhood's End* has become perhaps the most popular single book of science fiction today. It certainly outranks *More Than Human*.[5] Like that book, *Childhood's End* concerns the emergence of the next step in man's evolution, a step taken by children into a new species of telepathic communion and over-whelming telekinetic power. Clarke is perhaps even more insistent than Sturgeon on the importance, less the telepathy assumption, of the rule of normal science. Man is held in thrall by an advanced and astonishingly long-lived race called the "Overlords." Their technological power is awesome and, through Rikki Stormgren, the Secretary General of the United Nations, they rule earth utterly. Stormgren speaks with one Overlord only, Karellen.

> "You know why Wainwright [a religious leader] and his kind fear me, don't you?" asked Karellen. His voice was somber now, like a great organ rolling its notes from a high cathedral nave. "You will find men like him in all the world's religions. They know that we

[5] Jack Williamson, *Science Fiction Comes To College*, privately printed, 1971, p. 14.

represent reason and science, and, however, confident they may be in their beliefs, they fear that we will overthrow their gods. Not necessarily through any deliberate act, but in a subtler fashion. Science can destroy religion by ignoring it as well as by disproving its tenets. No one ever demonstrated, so far as I am aware, the nonexistence of Zeus or Thor, but they have few followers now. The Wainwrights fear, too, that we know the truth about the origins of their faiths. How long, they wonder, have we been observing humanity? Have we watched Mohammed begin the hegira, or Moses giving the Jews their laws? Do we know all that is false in the stories they believe?" [6]

Science is clearly central to this novel. The basis of the story is modern Darwinian evolution. The Overlords are nursemaids for the human race. Given current trends, Overlord science predicts, man will soon irradiate himself. Man, however, is potentially *Homo Gestalt* (though Clarke doesn't use this term) and for the sake of that newer man, Karellen and company control the life of current man. Like children, we are to be protected against ourselves. When "Total Breakthrough" occurs, when man's children suddenly all at once and everywhere on the planet, mutate into *Homo Gestalt*, we have childhood's end.

The relation between the Overlords and *Homo sapiens* is explained at length in terms of Darwinian evolution.

> ... there are many races in the universe, and some of them discovered these [telepathic] powers long before your species—or mine—appeared on the scene. They have been waiting for you to join them, and now the time has come ... probably, like most men, you have always regarded us as your masters. That is not true. We have never been more than guardians, doing a duty imposed upon us from—above. ... we are the midwives. But we ourselves are barren. (p. 176)

> "... we represent the ends of two different evolutions ... Our potentialities are exhausted, but yours are still untapped." (pp. 182–83)

The Overlords, not only to serve the "Overmind," but, in order to learn how they themselves might make Total Breakthrough, have

---

[6] Arthur C. Clarke, *Childhood's End*, Ballantine, New York, 1972 (1953), p. 23.

restrained and guided man for a hundred years. They have interdicted man's progress with the old antiscience fears of the nineteenth century—"The stars are not for man." (p. 137)—only to have man grow, under the rule of evolution, into a mind-thing that can inhabit the stars, or the voids between them, with perfect ease. Like Hip's role in *More Than Human*, the "epidemic" that affects all human children, but which can never affect the Overlords, shows ordinary man superior to his apparent master.

Unlike Sturgeon, Clarke reverses the science on which his book relies. Every student of evolution knows that although one species is thought to emerge by discontinuous mutation from the loins of a previous species, this is seen *always* as occurring in one individual at a time. If the trait is successful, then it spreads and eventually a new species emerges. Clarke throws all that to the winds and, despite talk about evolutionary lines, postulates the whole human race moving on into a new and perfectly communal era. Where the nagging doubt is scientized in Sturgeon, science is spiritualized in Clarke. From the standpoint of aesthetic unity within the decorum of the genre of Wellsian science fiction, Clarke's book is clearly inferior to Sturgeon's; from the standpoint of popularity, however, Sturgeon's book is just as clearly inferior to Clarke's. This relation between the two books can be explained by considering how each uses the fantastic.

Sturgeon uses the fantastic in the paradigmatic way prescribed for Wellsian science fiction. The world becomes ordered (as it does in fairy tales and detective fiction), that order taking its specific rules from the body of normal science known at the time of writing. Clarke, though still falling well within our general definition for science fiction, falls outside Wellsian science fiction by virtue of his rejection of the narratively operative assumption of modern evolution. This rejection, this sudden reversal of a ground rule of its narrative world, is a central episode in *Childhood's End*. This episode is paradigmatically fantastic. The astonishment of the adults at their mutated children provides signals enough. Somehow, this novel which is too fantastic to be pure science fiction, is a work of science fiction more popular than its better-done, award-winning parallel.

The particular fantasy that Clarke indulges is the Christian fantasy of the descent of Grace. The coming of Total Breakthrough, like the Second Coming, represents salvation for all men not already corrupt. Sturgeon and Clarke agree that children are innocent and adults corrupt. However, Sturgeon sees ordinary man achieving salvation through individual acts of bravery (as when Hip releases the lethal Gerry), while Clarke sees all men achieving salvation through divine intercession. Sturgeon's salvation is a creed for this world; Clarke's salvation is eschatological. *Childhood's End* is an aptly chosen title.

The notion of the Second Coming, the idea that God may intervene and save us all, gives rise to the antinomian heresy that we saw in C. S. Lewis' children's literature and that runs throughout the Fantasies of George MacDonald. North Wind tells Diamond that " 'I'm either not a dream, or there's something better that's not a dream.' " [7] When a father in *Childhood's End* is told about the dreams of one of his mutating children (mutating not at conception but after formation, thus again violating normal science), he remarks that "I never believed that they were simply the imaginings of a child. They were so incredible that—I know this sounds ridiculous—they *had* to be based on some reality" (p. 173). This is a faith in the "Aesthetics of Redemption." When Total Breakthrough occurs, the children of Man float off into space. They are, in terms of literary structural parallels, on their way to heaven.

Clark's work, then, shares something of the theology of the fantasist MacDonald, although its readiest generic label and its most visible structural features align it with Sturgeon. When we recognize the religious understructure of *Childhood's End*, we change the emphasis we put on individual incidents. For example, when read as a story of quasi-scientific, utopian science fiction, the incidents centering on Stormgren seem to be merely embellishments, games played with characterization to humanize the tale. However, viewed as a rewrite of the Bible, this judgment changes. When Stormgren is near death, he visits Karellen for the last time. They have always spoken through a one-way window and no man has ever (to that point) looked upon an Overlord. Stormgren, the faithful servant, asks that he be allowed this. At the end of the interview, for the first time, a light comes on on Karellen's side of

[7] George MacDonald, *At the Back of the North Wind*, Airmont, New York, 1966 (1871), p. 275.

the window: a chair, twice the size of a man, and, just going through a closing door, the back of a being! Stormgren is grateful for this privileged glimpse, muses on Karellen's guardianship, and hopes that in the future when Karellen can come to earth he will "stand beside the grave of the first man ever to be his friend" (pp. 64–5). In Exodus, God and Moses argue frequently about the best way to educate those foolish people who will persist in making golden calves. Moses says,

> I beseech thee, shew me thy glory ... And he said, Thou canst not see my face: for there shall no man see me, and live.
>
> And the Lord said, Behold, *there* is a place by me, and thou shalt stand upon a rock:
>
> And it shall come to pass, while my glory passeth by, that I will put thee in a clift of the rock, and will cover thee with my hand while I pass by:
>
> And I will take away mine hand, and thou shalt see my back parts: but my face shall not be seen. (Exodus 33: 18–23)

Judged by the standards of Wellsian science fiction, *More Than Human* is a better book than *Childhood's End*. This is so precisely because Clarke's novel is in a significant regard the more fantastic. Once the narrative ground rules are created, the fantastic is proscribed from Wellsian science fiction. However, Clarke's book is by far the more popular. It would seem that either we throw out the notion of the aesthetic importance of organic unity or else we recognize that our genre label of *science fiction* has led us astray. This latter conclusion, of course, is the correct one. Within the decorum of the more fantastic *Childhood's End*, Clarke creates an organic unity every bit as complete as Sturgeon's. One should recall that Karellen's voice is initially described as "like a great organ rolling its notes from a high cathedral nave." Clarke has, by participation in the structures and images of Christianity, prepared us well for the Second Coming, for Total Breakthrough, and when it comes this fantastic event may contradict normal science, but it is easily accommodated by a reader trained in the underlying image structure of the book. Perhaps because the hope that Christianity— and Clarke—holds out is such a wholesome hope, the flawed science fiction is perceived as the better fiction.

This comparison indicates that genre labels, even when carefully attached to definitions, may play us false. In this example, it was important to know not only that these works were science fictions but that one was more fantastic than the other. Further, by comparing the use of the fantastic not to another work in the genre but to another work (Exodus) that makes the same use of the fantastic, we can better understand how Clarke's book functions, better see its hidden artistry, and better understand its affects on a large readership.

One can imagine a *continuum of the fantastic* that arranges all works within the genre of science fiction according to their degree of use of the fantastic. At one end of the scale we find *I, Robot*, at the other *A Voyage to Arcturus*. This exercise in arrangement is hardly frivolous. Just as the application of genre distinctions has often led readers to new insights about literature, so application of continuum distinctions may also, as in the Sturgeon/Clarke comparison, yield new insights also, insights that directly complement those of normal genre criticism.

On Science Fiction

by C. S. Lewis

Sometimes a village or small town which we have known all our lives becomes the scene of a murder, a novel, or a centenary, and then for a few months everyone knows its name and crowds go to visit it. A like thing happens to one's private recreations. I had been walking, and reading Trollope, for years when I found myself suddenly overtaken, as if by a wave from behind, by a boom in Trollope and a short-lived craze for what was called hiking. And lately I have had the same sort of experience again. I had read fantastic fiction of all sorts ever since I could read, including, of course, the particular kind which Wells practised in his *Time Machine*, *First Men in the Moon* and others. Then, some fifteen or twenty years ago, I became aware of a bulge in the production of such stories. In America whole magazines began to be exclusively devoted to them. The execution was usually detestable; the conceptions, sometimes worthy of better treatment. About this time the name *scientifiction*, soon altered to *science fiction*, began to be common. Then, perhaps five or six years ago, the bulge still continuing and even increasing, there was an improvement: not that very bad stories ceased to be the majority, but that the good ones became better and more numerous. It was after this that the *genre* began to attract the attention (always, I think, contemptuous) of the literary weeklies. There seems, in fact, to be a double paradox in its history: it began to be popular when it least deserved popularity, and to excite critical contempt as soon as it ceased to be wholly contemptible.

Of the articles I have read on the subject (and I expect I have

"On Science Fiction" by C. S. Lewis. From *Of Other Worlds: Essays and Stories*, by C. S. Lewis, edited by Walter Hooper (New York: Harcourt, Brace and World, 1967), pp. 59–73. Copyright © 1966 by The Executors of the Estate of C. S. Lewis. Reprinted by permission of Harcourt Brace Jovanovich, Inc. and William Collins Sons & Co. Ltd.

missed many) I do not find that I can make any use. For one thing, most were not very well informed. For another, many were by people who clearly hated the kind they wrote about. It is very dangerous to write about a kind you hate. Hatred obscures all distinctions. I don't like detective stories and therefore all detective stories look much alike to me: if I wrote about them I should therefore infallibly write drivel. Criticism of kinds, as distinct from criticism of works, cannot of course be avoided: I shall be driven to criticize one sub-species of science fiction myself. But it is, I think, the most subjective and least reliable type of criticism. Above all, it should not masquerade as criticism of individual works. Many reviews are useless because, while purporting to condemn the book, they only reveal the reviewer's dislike of the kind to which it belongs. Let bad tragedies be censured by those who love tragedy, and bad detective stories by those who love the detective story. Then we shall learn their real faults. Otherwise we shall find epics blamed for not being novels, farces for not being high comedies, novels by James for lacking the swift action of Smollett. Who wants to hear a particular claret abused by a fanatical teetotaller, or a particular woman by a confirmed misogynist?

Moreover, most of these articles were chiefly concerned to account for the bulge in the output and consumption of science fiction on sociological and psychological grounds. This is of course a perfectly legitimate attempt. But here as elsewhere those who hate the thing they are trying to explain are not perhaps those most likely to explain it. If you have never enjoyed a thing and do not know what it feels like to enjoy it, you will hardly know what sort of people go to it, in what moods, seeking what sort of gratification. And if you do not know what sort of people they are, you will be ill-equipped to find out what conditions have made them so. In this way, one may say of a kind not only (as Wordsworth says of the poet) that "you must love it ere to you it will seem worthy of your love," but that you must at least have loved it once if you are even to warn others against it. Even if it is a vice to read science fiction, those who cannot understand the very temptation to that vice will not be likely to tell us anything of value about it. Just as I, for instance, who have no taste for cards, could not find anything very useful to say by way of warning against deep play. They will be like the frigid preaching chastity, misers warning us against prodigality, cowards denouncing rashness. And because, as I have said, hatred assimilates all the hated objects, it will make you assume that all the things lumped together as science fiction are of the same sort, and that the psychology of all those who like to read any of them is the same. That is likely to make the problem of explaining the bulge seem simpler than it really is.

I myself shall not attempt to explain it at all. I am not interested in the bulge. It is nothing to me whether a given work makes part of it or was written long before it occurred. The existence of the bulge cannot make the kind (or kinds) intrinsically better or worse; though of course bad specimens will occur most often within it.

I will now try to divide this species of narrative into its sub-species. I shall begin with that sub-species which I think radically bad, in order to get it out of our way.

In this sub-species the author leaps forward into an imagined future when planetary, sidereal, or even galactic travel has become common. Against this huge backcloth he then proceeds to develop an ordinary love-story, spy-story, wreck-story, or crime-story. This seems to me tasteless. Whatever in a work of art is not used, is doing harm. The faintly imagined, and sometimes strictly unimaginable, scene and properties, only blur the real theme and distract us from any interest it might have had. I presume that the authors of such stories are, so to speak, Displaced Persons—commercial authors who did not really want to write science fiction at all, but who availed themselves of its popularity by giving a veneer of science fiction to their normal kind of work. But we must distinguish. A leap into the future, a rapid assumption of all the changes which are feigned to have occurred, is a legitimate "machine" if it enables the author to develop a story of real value which could not have been told (or not so economically) in any other way. Thus John Collier in *Tom's A-Cold* (1933) wants to write a story of heroic action among people themselves semi-barbarous but supported by the surviving tradition of a literate culture recently overthrown. He could, of course, find an historical situation suitable to his purpose, somewhere in the early Dark Ages. But that would involve all manner of archaeological details which would spoil his book if they were done perfunctorily and perhaps distract our interest if they were done well. He is therefore, on my view, fully justified in positing such a state of affairs in England after the destruction of our present civilization. That enables him (and us) to assume a familiar climate, flora, and fauna. He is not interested in the process whereby the change came about. That is all over before the curtain rises. This supposition is equivalent to the rules of his game: criticism applies only to the quality of his play. A much more frequent use of the leap into the future, in our time, is satiric or prophetic: the author criticizes tendencies in the present by imagining them carried out ("produced," as Euclid would say) to their logical limit. *Brave New World* and *Nineteen Eighty-Four* leap to our minds. I can see no objection to such a "machine." Nor do I see much use in discussing, as someone did, whether books that use it can be called "novels" or not. That is merely a question of definition. You may define the novel either so as to exclude or so as to include them. The best definition is that which proves itself most convenient. And of course to devise a definition for the purpose of excluding either *The Waves* in one direction or *Brave New World* in another, and then blame them for being excluded, is foolery.

I am, then, condemning not all books which suppose a future widely different from the present, but those which do so without a good reason, which leap a thousand years to find plots and passions which they could have found at home.

Having condemned that sub-species, I am glad to turn to another which I believe to be legitimate, though I have not the slightest taste for it myself. If the former is the fiction of the Displaced Persons, this might be called the fiction of Engineers. It is written by people who are primarily interested in space-travel, or in other undiscovered techniques, as real possibilities in the actual universe. They give us in imaginative form their guesses as to how the thing might be done. Jules Verne's *Twenty Thousand Leagues Under the Sea* and Wells's *Land Ironclads* were once specimens of this kind, though the coming of the real submarine and the real tank has altered their original interest. Arthur Clarke's *Prelude to Space* is another. I am too uneducated scientifically to criticize such stories on the mechanical side; and I am so completely out of sympathy with the projects they anticipate that I am incapable of criticizing them as stories. I am as blind to their appeal as a pacifist is to *Maldon* and *Lepanto*, or an aristocratophobe (if I may coin the word) to the *Arcadia*. But heaven forbid that I should regard the limitations of my sympathy as anything save a red light which warns me not to criticize at all. For all I know, these may be very good stories in their own kind.

I think it useful to distinguish from these Engineers' Stories a third sub-species where the interest is, in a sense, scientific, but speculative. When we learn from the sciences the probable nature of places or conditions which no human being has experienced, there is, in normal men, an impulse to attempt to imagine them. Is any man such a dull clod that he can look at the moon through a good telescope without asking himself what it would be like to walk among those mountains under that black, crowded sky? The scientists themselves, the moment they go beyond purely mathematical statements, can hardly avoid describing the facts in terms of their probable effect on the senses of a human observer. Prolong this, and give, along with that observer's sense experience, his probable emotions and thoughts, and you at once have a rudimentary science fiction. And of course men have been doing this for centuries. What would Hades be like if you could go there alive? Homer sends Odysseus there and gives his answer. Or again, what would it be like at the Antipodes? (For this was a question of the same sort so long as men believed that the torrid zone rendered them forever inaccessible.) Dante takes you there: he describes with all the gusto of the later scientifictionist how surprising it was to see the sun in such an unusual position. Better still, what would it be like if you could get to the centre of the earth? Dante tells you at the end of the *Inferno* where he and Virgil, after climbing down from the shoulders to the waist of Lucifer, find that they have to climb up from his waist to his feet, because of course they have passed the centre of gravitation. It is a perfect science fiction effect. Thus again Athanasius Kircher in his *Iter Extaticum Celeste* (1656) will take you to all the planets and most of the stars, presenting as vividly as he can what you would see and feel if this were possible. He, like Dante, uses supernatural means of transport. In Wells's *First Men in the Moon* we have means which are feigned to be natural. What keeps his story within this sub-species, and distinguishes it from those of the Engineers, is his choice of a quite impossible composition called cavorite. This impossibility is of course a merit, not a defect. A man of his ingenuity could easily have thought up something more plausible. But the more plausible, the worse. That would merely invite interest in actual possibilities of reaching the Moon, an interest foreign to his story. Never mind how they got there; we are imagining what it would be like. The first glimpse of the unveiled airless sky, the lunar landscape, the lunar levity, the incomparable solitude, then the growing terror, finally the over-whelming approach of the lunar night—it is for these things that the story (especially in its original and shorter form) exists.

How anyone can think this form illegitimate or contemptible passes my understanding. It may very well be convenient not to call such things novels. If you prefer, call them a very special form of novels. Either way, the conclusion will be much the same: they are to be tried by their own rules. It is absurd to condemn them because they do not often display any deep or sensitive characterization. They oughtn't to. It is a fault if they do. Wells's Cavor and Bedford have rather too much than too little character. Every good writer knows that the more unusual the scenes and events of his story are, the slighter, the more ordinary, the more typical his persons should be. Hence Gulliver is a commonplace little man and Alice a commonplace little girl. If they had been more remarkable they would have wrecked their books. The Ancient Mariner himself is a very ordinary man. To tell how odd things struck odd people is to have an oddity too much: he who is to see strange sights must not himself be strange. He ought to be as nearly as possible Everyman or Anyman. Of course, we must not confuse slight or typical characterization with impossible or unconvincing characterization. Falsification of character will always spoil a story. But character can apparently be reduced, simplified, to almost any extent with wholly satisfactory results. The greater ballads are an instance.

Of course, a given reader may be (some readers seem to be) interested in nothing else in the world except detailed studies of complex human personalities. If so, he has a good reason for not reading those kinds of work which neither demand nor admit it. He has no reason for condemning them, and indeed no qualification for speaking of them at all. We must not allow the novel of manners to give laws to all literature: let it rule its own domain. We must not listen to Pope's maxim about the proper study of mankind. The proper study of man is everything. The proper study of man as artist is everything which gives a foothold to the imagination and the passions.

But while I think this sort of science fiction legitimate, and capable of great virtues, it is not a kind which can endure copious production. It is only the first visit to the Moon or to Mars that is, for this purpose, any good. After each has been discovered in one or two stories (and turned out to be different in each) it becomes difficult to suspend our disbelief in favour of subsequent stories. However good they were they would kill each other by becoming numerous.

My next sub-species is what I would call the Eschatological. It is about the future, but not in the same way as *Brave New World* or *The Sleeper Awakes*. They were political or social. This kind gives an imaginative vehicle to speculations about the ultimate destiny of our species. Examples are Wells's *Time Machine*, Olaf Stapledon's *Last and First Men*, or Arthur Clarke's *Childhood's End.* It is here that a definition of science fiction which separates it entirely from the novel becomes imperative. The form of *Last and First Men* is not novelistic at all. It is indeed in a new form—the pseudo history. The pace, the concern with broad, general movements, the tone, are all those of the historiographer, not the novelist. It was the right form for the theme. And since we are here diverging so widely from the novel, I myself would gladly include in this sub-species a work which is not even narrative, Geoffrey Dennis's *The End of the World* (1930). And I would certainly include, from J. B. S. Haldane's *Possible Worlds* (1927), the brilliant, though to my mind depraved, paper called "The Last Judgement."

Work of this kind gives expression to thoughts and emotions which I think it good that we should sometimes entertain. It is sobering and cathartic to remember, now and then, our collective smallness, our apparent isolation, the apparent indifference of nature, the slow biological, geological, and astronomical processes which may, in the long run, make many of our hopes (possibly some of our fears) ridiculous. If *memento mori* is sauce for the individual, I do not know why the species should be spared the taste of it. Stories of this kind may explain the hardly disguised political rancour which I thought I detected in one article on science fiction. The insinuation was that those who read or wrote it were probably Fascists. What lurks behind such a hint is, I suppose, something like this. If we were all on board ship and there was trouble among the stewards, I can just conceive their chief spokesman looking with disfavour on anyone who stole away from the fierce debates in the saloon or pantry to take a breather on deck. For up there, he would taste the salt, he would see the vastness of the water, he would re-member that the ship had a whither and a whence. He would remember things like fog, storms, and ice. What had seemed, in the hot, lighted rooms down below to be merely the scene for a political crisis, would appear once more as a tiny egg-shell moving rapidly through an immense darkness over an element in which man cannot live. It would not necessarily change his convictions about the rights and wrongs of the dispute down below, but it would probably show them in a new light. It could hardly fail to remind him that the stewards were taking for granted hopes more momentous than that of a rise in pay, and the passengers forgetting dangers more serious than that of having to cook and serve their own meals. Stories of the sort I am describing are like that visit to the deck. They cool us. They are as refreshing as that passage in E. M. Forster where the man, looking at the monkeys, realizes that most of the inhabitants of India do not care how India is governed. Hence the uneasiness which they arouse in those who, for whatever reason, wish to keep us wholly imprisoned in the immediate conflict. That perhaps is why people are so ready with the charge of "escape." I never fully understood it till my friend Professor Tolkien asked me the very simple question, "What class of men would you expect to be most preoccupied with, and most hostile to, the idea of escape?" and gave the obvious answer: jailers. The charge of Fascism is, to be sure, mere mud-flinging. Fascists, as well as Communists, are jailers; both would assure us that the proper study of prisoners is prison. But there is perhaps this truth behind it: that those who brood much on the remote past or future, or stare long at the night sky, are less likely than others to be ardent or orthodox partisans.

I turn at last to that sub-species in which alone I myself am greatly interested. It is best approached by reminding ourselves of a fact which every writer on the subject whom I have read completely ignores. Far the best of the American magazines bears the significant title *Fantasy and Science Fiction*. In it (as also in many other publications of the same type) you will find not only stories about space-travel but stories about gods, ghosts, ghouls, demons, fairies, monsters, etc. This gives us our clue. The last sub-species of science fiction represents simply an imaginative impulse as old as the human race working under the special conditions of our own time. It is not difficult to see why those who wish to visit strange regions in search of such beauty, awe, or terror as the actual world does not supply have increasingly been driven to other planets or other stars. It is the result of increasing geographical knowledge. The less known the real world is, the more plausibly your marvels can be located near at hand. As the area of knowledge spreads, you need to go further afield: like a man moving his house further and further out into the country as the new building estates catch him up. Thus in Grimm's *Märchen*, stories told by peasants in wooded country, you need only walk an hour's journey into the next forest to find a home for your witch or ogre. The author of *Beowulf* can put Grendel's lair in a place of which he himself says *Nis paet feor heonon Mil-gemearces.* Homer, writing for a maritime people has to take Odysseus several days' journey by sea before he meets Circe, Calypso, the Cyclops, or the Sirens. Old Irish has a form called the *immram,* a voyage among islands. Arthurian romance, oddly at first sight, seems usually content with the old *Märchen* machine of a neighbouring forest. Chrétien and his successors knew a great deal of real geography. Perhaps the explanation is that these romances are chiefly written by Frenchmen about Britain, and Britain in the past. *Huon of Bordeaux* places Oberon in the East. Spenser invents a country not in our universe at all; Sidney goes to an imaginary past in Greece. By the eighteenth century we have to move well out into the country. Paltock and Swift take us to remote seas, Voltaire to America. Rider Haggard had to go to unexplored Africa or Tibet; Bulwer Lytton, to the depths of the Earth. It might have been predicted that stories of this kind would, sooner or later, have to leave Tellus altogether. We know now that where Haggard put She and Kôr we should really find groundnut schemes or Mau Mau.

In this kind of story the pseudo-scientific apparatus is to be taken simply as a "machine" in the sense which that word bore for the Neo-Classical critics. The most superficial appearance of plausibility—the merest sop to our critical intellect—will do. I am inclined to think that frankly supernatural methods are best. I took a hero once to Mars in a space-ship, but when I knew better I had angels convey him to Venus. Nor need the strange worlds, when we get there, be at all strictly tied to scientific probabilities. It is their wonder, or beauty, or suggestiveness that matter. When I myself put canals on Mars I believe I already knew that better telescopes had dissipated that old optical delusion. The point was that they were part of the Martian myth as it already existed in the common mind.

The defence and analysis of this kind are, accordingly, no different from those of fantastic or mythopoeic literature in general. But here sub-species and sub-sub-species break out in baffling multitude. The impossible—or things so immensely improbable that they have, imaginatively, the same status as the impossible—can be used in literature for many different purposes. I cannot hope to do more than suggest a few main types: the subject still awaits its Aristotle.

It may represent the intellect, almost completely free from emotion, at play. The purest specimen would be Abbott's *Flatland*, though even here some emotion arises from the sense (which it inculcates) of our own limitations—the consciousness that our own human awareness of the world is arbitrary and contingent. Sometimes such play gives a pleasure analogous to that of the conceit. I have unluckily forgotten both the name and author of my best example: the story of a man who is enabled to travel into the future, because himself, in that future when he shall have discovered a method of time travel, comes back to himself in the present (then, of course, the past) and fetches him.[1] Less comic, but a more strenuous game, is the very fine working out of the logical consequences of time-travel in Charles Williams's *Many Dimensions*: where, however, this element is combined with many others.

Secondly, the impossible may be simply a postulate to liberate farcical consequences, as in 'F. Anstey's' *Brass Bottle*. The garunda-stone in his *Vice Versa* is not so pure an example; a serious moral and, indeed, something not far from pathos, come in—perhaps against the author's wish.

Sometimes it is a postulate which liberates consequences very far from comic, and, when this is so, if the story is good it will usually point a moral, of itself, without any didactic manipulation by the author on the conscious level. Stevenson's *Dr Jekyll and Mr Hyde* would be an example. Another is Marc Brandel's *Cast the First*

---

[1] [Lewis is thinking, I believe, of Robert A. Heinlein's "By His Bootstraps" in *Spectrum: A Science Fiction Anthology* (1961).—Walter Hooper.]

Shadow, where a man, long solitary, despised, and oppressed, because he had no shadow, at last meets a woman who shares his innocent defect, but later turns from her in disgust and indignation on finding that she has, in addition, the loathsome and unnatural property of having no reflection. Readers who do not write themselves often describe such stories as allegories, but I doubt if it is as allegories that they arise in the author's mind.

In all these the impossibility is, as I have said, a postulate, something to be granted before the story gets going. Within that frame we inhabit the known world and are as realistic as anyone else. But in the next type (and the last I shall deal with) the marvellous is in the grain of the whole work. We are, throughout, in another world. What makes that world valuable is not, of course, mere multiplication of the marvellous either for comic effect (as in *Baron Munchausen* and sometimes in Ariosto and Boiardo) or for mere astonishment (as, I think, in the worst of the *Arabian Nights* or in some children's stories), but its quality, its flavour. If good novels are comments on life, good stories of this sort (which are very much rarer) are actual additions to life; they give, like certain rare dreams, sensations we never had before, and enlarge our conception of the range of possible experience. Hence the difficulty of discussing them at all with those who refuse to be taken out of what they call "real life"—which means, perhaps, the groove through some far wider area of possible experience to which our senses and our biological, social, or economic interests usually confine us—or, if taken, can see nothing outside it but aching boredom or sickening monstrosity. They shudder and ask to go home. Specimens of this kind, at its best, will never be common. I would include parts of the *Odyssey*, the *Hymn to Aphrodite*, much of the *Kalevala* and *The Faerie Queene*, some of Malory (but none of Malory's best work) and more of *Huon*, parts of Novalis's *Heinrich von Ofterdingen*, *The Ancient Mariner* and *Christabel*, Beckford's *Vathek*, Morris's *Jason* and the *Prologue* (little else) of the *Earthly Paradise*, MacDonald's *Phantastes*, *Lilith*, and *The Golden Key*, Eddison's *Worm Ouroboros*, Tolkien's *Lord of the Rings*, and that shattering, intolerable, and irresistible work, David Lindsay's *Voyage to Arcturus*. Also Mervyn Peake's *Titus Groan*. Some of Ray Bradbury's stories perhaps make the grade. W. H. Hodgson's *The Night Land* would have made it in eminence from the unforgettable sombre splendour of the images it presents, if it were not disfigured by a sentimental and irrelevant erotic interest and by a foolish, and flat archaism of style. (I do not mean that all archaism is foolish, and have never seen the modern hatred of it cogently defended. If archaism succeeds in giving us the sense of having entered a remote world, it justifies itself. Whether it is correct by philological standards does not then matter a rap.)

I am not sure that anyone has satisfactorily explained the keen, lasting, and solemn pleasure which such stories can give. Jung, who went furthest, seems to me to produce as his explanation one more myth which affects us in the same way as the rest. Surely the analysis of water should not itself be wet? I shall not attempt to do what Jung failed to do. But I would like to draw attention to a neglected fact: the astonishing intensity of the dislike which some readers feel for the mythopoeic. I first found it out by accident. A lady (and, what makes the story more piquant, she herself was a Jungian psychologist by profession) had been talking about a dreariness which seemed to be creeping over her life, the drying up in her of the power to feel pleasure, the aridity of her mental landscape. Drawing a bow at a venture, I asked, "Have you any taste for fantasies and fairy tales?" I shall never forget how her muscles tightened, her hands clenched themselves, her eyes started as if with horror, and her voice changed, as she hissed out, "I *loathe* them." Clearly we here have to do not with a critical opinion but with something like a phobia. And I have seen traces of it elsewhere, though never quite so violent. On the other side, I know from my own experience, that those who like the mythopoeic like it with almost equal intensity. The two phenomena, taken together, should at least dispose of the theory that it is something trivial. It would seem from the reactions it produces, that the mythopoeic is rather, for good or ill, a mode of imagination which does something to us at a deep level. If some seem to go to it in almost compulsive need, others seem to be in terror of what they may meet there. But that is of course only suspicion. What I feel far more sure of is the critical *caveat* which I propounded a while ago. Do not criticize what you have no taste for without great caution. And above all, do not ever criticize what you simply can't stand. I will lay all the cards on the table. I have long since discovered my own private *phobia,* the thing I can't bear in literature, the thing which makes me profoundly uncomfortable, is the representation of anything like a quasi love affair between two children. It embarrasses and nauseates me. But of course I regard this not as a charter to write slashing reviews of books in which the hated theme occurs, but as a warning not to pass judgement on them at all. For my reaction is unreasonable: such child-loves quite certainly occur in real life and I can give no reason why they should not be represented in art. If they touch the scar of some early *trauma* in me, that is my misfortune. And I would venture to advise all who are attempting to become critics to adopt the same principle. A violent and actually resentful reaction to all books of a certain kind, or to situations of a certain kind, is a danger signal. For I am convinced that good adverse criticism is the most difficult thing we have to do. I would advise everyone to begin it under the most favourable conditions: that is, where you thoroughly know and heartily like the thing the author is trying to do, and have enjoyed many books where it was done well. Then you will have some chance of really showing that he has failed and perhaps even of showing why. But if our real reaction to a book is "Ugh! I just can't bear this sort of thing," then I think we shall not be able to diagnose whatever real faults it has. We may labour to conceal our emotion, but we shall end in a welter of emotive, unanalysed, vogue-words—"arch," "facetious," "bogus," "adolescent," "immature," and the rest. When we really know what is wrong we need none of these.

The Imagination of Disaster

by Susan Sontag

The typical science fiction film has a form as predictable as a Western, and is made up of elements which, to a practiced eye, are as classic as the saloon brawl, the blonde schoolteacher from the East, and the gun duel on the deserted main street.

One model scenario proceeds through five phases.

(1) The arrival of the thing. (Emergence of the monsters, landing of the alien spaceship, etc.) This is usually witnessed or suspected by just one person, a young scientist on a field trip. Nobody, neither his neighbors nor his colleagues, will believe him for some time. The hero is not married, but has a sympathetic though also incredulous girl friend.

(2) Confirmation of the hero's report by a host of witnesses to a great act of destruction. (If the invaders are beings from another planet, a fruitless attempt to parley with them and get them to leave peacefully.) The local police are summoned to deal with the situation and massacred.

(3) In the capital of the country, conferences between scientists and the military take place, with the hero lecturing before a chart, map, or blackboard. A national emergency is declared. Reports of further destruction. Authorities from other countries arrive in black limousines. All international tensions are suspended in view of the planetary emergency. This stage often includes a rapid montage of news broadcasts in various languages, a meeting at the UN, and more conferences between the military and the scientists. Plans are made for destroying the enemy.

(4) Further atrocities. At some point the hero's girl friend is in grave danger. Massive counter-attacks by international forces, with

brilliant displays of rocketry, rays, and other advanced weapons, are all unsuccessful. Enormous military casualties, usually by incineration. Cities are destroyed and/or evacuated. There is an obligatory scene here of panicked crowds stampeding along a highway or a big bridge, being waved on by numerous policemen who, if the film is Japanese, are immaculately white-gloved, preternaturally calm, and call out in dubbed English, "Keep moving. There is no need to be alarmed."

(5) More conferences, whose motif is: "They must be vulnerable to something." Throughout the hero has been working in his lab to this end. The final strategy, upon which all hopes depend, is drawn up; the ultimate weapon—often a super-powerful, as yet untested, nuclear device—is mounted. Countdown. Final repulse of the monster or invaders. Mutual congratulations, while the hero and girl friend embrace cheek to cheek and scan the skies sturdily. "But have we seen the last of them?"

The film I have just described should be in Technicolor and on a wide screen. Another typical scenario, which follows, is simpler and suited to black-and-white films with a lower budget. It has four phases.

(1) The hero (usually, but not always, a scientist) and his girl friend, or his wife and two children, are disporting themselves in some innocent ultra-normal middle-class surroundings—their house in a small town, or on vacation (camping, boating). Suddenly, someone starts behaving strangely; or some innocent form of vegetation becomes monstrously enlarged and ambulatory. If a character is pictured driving an automobile, something gruesome looms up in the middle of the road. If it is night, strange lights hurtle across the sky.

(2) After following the thing's tracks, or determining that It is radioactive, or poking around a huge crater—in short, conducting some sort of crude investigation—the hero tries to warn the local authorities, without effect; nobody believes anything is amiss. The hero knows better. If the thing is tangible, the house is elaborately barricaded. If the invading alien is an invisible parasite, a doctor or friend is called in, who is himself rather quickly killed or "taken possession of" by the thing.

(3) The advice of whoever further is consulted proves useless.

Meanwhile, It continues to claim other victims in the town, which remains implausibly isolated from the rest of the world. General helplessness.

(4) One of two possibilities. Either the hero prepares to do battle alone, accidentally discovers the thing's one vulnerable point, and destroys it. Or, he somehow manages to get out of town and succeeds in laying his case before competent authorities. They, along the lines of the first script but abridged, deploy a complex technology which (after initial setbacks) finally prevails against the invaders.

Another version of the second script opens with the scientist-hero in his laboratory, which is located in the basement or on the grounds of his tasteful, prosperous house. Through his experiments, he unwittingly causes a frightful metamorphosis in some class of plants or animals which turn carnivorous and go on a rampage. Or else, his experiments have caused him to be injured (sometimes irrevocably) or "invaded" himself. Perhaps he has been experimenting with radiation, or has built a machine to communicate with beings from other planets or transport him to other places or times.

Another version of the first script involves the discovery of some fundamental alteration in the conditions of existence of our planet, brought about by nuclear testing, which will lead to the extinction in a few months of all human life. For example: the temperature of the earth is becoming too high or too low to support life, or the earth is cracking in two, or it is gradually being blanketed by lethal fallout.

A third script, somewhat but not altogether different from the first two, concerns a journey through space—to the moon, or some other planet. What the space-voyagers discover commonly is that the alien terrain is in a state of dire emergency, itself threatened by extra-planetary invaders or nearing extinction through the practice of nuclear warfare. The terminal dramas of the first and second scripts are played out there, to which is added the problem of getting away from the doomed and/or hostile planet and back to Earth.

I am aware, of course, that there are thousands of science fiction novels (their heyday was the late 1940s), not to mention the transcriptions of science fiction themes which, more and more, provide the principal subject-matter of comic books. But I propose to discuss science fiction films (the present period began in 1950 and continues, considerably abated, to this day) as an independent subgenre, without reference to other media—and, most particularly, without reference to the novels from which, in many cases, they were adapted. For, while novel and film may share the same plot, the fundamental difference between the resources of the novel and the film makes them quite dissimilar.

Certainly, compared with the science fiction novels, their film counterparts have unique strengths, one of which is the immediate representation of the extraordinary: physical deformity and mutation, missile and rocket combat, toppling skyscrapers. The movies are, naturally, weak just where the science fiction novels (some of them) are strong—on science. But in place of an intellectual workout, they can supply something the novels can never provide—sensuous elaboration. In the films it is by means of images and sounds, not words that have to be translated by the imagination, that one can participate in the fantasy of living through one's own death and more, the death of cities, the destruction of humanity itself.

Science fiction films are not about science. They are about disaster, which is one of the oldest subjects of art. In science fiction films disaster is rarely viewed intensively; it is always extensive. It is a matter of quantity and ingenuity. If you will, it is a question of scale. But the scale, particularly in the wide-screen Technicolor films (of which the ones by the Japanese director Inoshiro Honda and the American director George Pal are technically the most convincing and visually the most exciting), does raise the matter to another level.

Thus, the science fiction film (like that of a very different contemporary genre, the Happening) is concerned with the aesthetics of destruction, with the peculiar beauties to be found in wreaking havoc, making a mess. And it is in the imagery of destruction that the core of a good science fiction film lies. Hence, the disadvantage of the cheap film—in which the monster appears or the rocket lands in a small dull-looking town. (Hollywood budget needs usually dictate that the town be in the Arizona or California desert. In *The Thing From Another World* [1951] the rather sleazy and confined set is supposed to be an encampment near the North Pole.) Still, good black-and-white science fiction films have been made. But a bigger budget, which usually means Technicolor, allows a much greater play back and forth among several model environments. There is the populous city. There is the lavish but ascetic interior of the spaceship—either the invaders' or ours—replete with streamlined chromium fixtures and dials and machines whose complexity is indicated by the number of colored lights they flash and strange noises they emit. There is the laboratory crowded with formidable boxes and scientific apparatus. There is a comparatively old-fashioned-looking conference room, where the scientists unfurl charts to explain the desperate state of things to the military. And each of these standard locales or backgrounds is subject to two modalities—intact and destroyed. We may, if we are lucky, be treated to a panorama of melting tanks, flying bodies, crashing walls, awesome craters and fissures in the earth, plummeting spacecraft, colorful deadly rays; and to a symphony of screams, weird electronic signals, the noisiest military hardware going, and the leaden tones of the laconic denizens of alien planets and their subjugated earthlings.

Certain of the primitive gratifications of science fiction films—for instance, the depiction of urban disaster on a colossally magnified scale—are shared with other types of films. Visually there is little difference between mass havoc as represented in the old horror and monster films and what we find in science fiction films, except (again) scale. In the old monster films, the monster always headed for the great city, where he had to do a fair bit of rampaging, hurling busses off bridges, crumpling trains in his bare hands, toppling buildings, and so forth. The archetype is King Kong, in Schoedsack's great film of 1933, running amok, first in the African village (trampling babies, a bit of footage excised from most prints), then in New York. This is really no different in spirit from the scene in Inoshiro Honda's *Rodan* (1957) in which two giant reptiles—with a wingspan of 500 feet and supersonic speeds—by flapping their wings whip up a cyclone that blows most of Tokyo to smithereens. Or the destruction of half of Japan by the gigantic robot with the great incinerating ray that shoots forth from his eyes, at the beginning of Honda's *The Mysterians* (1959). Or, the devastation by the rays from a fleet of flying saucers of New York, Paris, and Tokyo, in *Battle in Outer Space* (1960). Or, the inundation of New York in *When Worlds Collide* (1951). Or, the end of London in 1966 depicted in George Pal's *The Time Machine* (1960). Neither do these sequences differ in aesthetic intention from the destruction scenes in the big sword, sandal, and orgy color spectaculars set in Biblical and Roman times—the end of Sodom in Aldrich's *Sodom and Gomorrah*, of Gaza in De Mille's *Samson and Delilah*, of Rhodes in *The Colossus of Rhodes*, and of Rome in a dozen Nero movies. Griffith began it with the Babylon sequence in *Intolerance*, and to this day there is nothing like the thrill of watching all those expensive sets come tumbling down.

In other respects as well, the science fiction films of the 1950s take up familiar themes. The famous 1930s movie serials and comics of the adventures of Flash Gordon and Buck Rogers, as well as the more recent spate of comic book super-heroes with extraterrestrial origins (the most famous is Superman, a foundling from the planet Krypton, currently described as having been exploded by a nuclear blast), share motifs with more recent science fiction movies. But there is an important difference. The old science fiction films, and most of the comics, still have an essentially innocent relation to disaster. Mainly they offer new versions of the oldest romance of all—of the strong invulnerable hero with a mysterious lineage come to do battle on behalf of good and against evil. Recent science fiction films have a decided grimness, bolstered by their much greater degree of visual credibility, which contrasts strongly with the older films. Modern historical reality has greatly enlarged the imagination of disaster, and the protagonists—perhaps by the very nature of what is visited upon them—no longer seem wholly innocent.

The lure of such generalized disaster as a fantasy is that it releases one from normal obligations. The trump card of the end-of-the-world movies—like *The Day the Earth Caught Fire* (1962)—is that great scene with New York or London or Tokyo discovered empty, its entire population annihilated. Or, as in *The World, The Flesh, and The Devil* (1957), the whole movie can be devoted to the fantasy of occupying the deserted metropolis and starting all over again, a world Robinson Crusoe.

Another kind of satisfaction these films supply is extreme moral simplification—that is to say, a morally acceptable fantasy where one can give outlet to cruel or at least amoral feelings. In this respect, science fiction films partly overlap with horror films. This is the undeniable pleasure we derive from looking at freaks, beings excluded from the category of the human. The sense of superiority over the freak conjoined in varying proportions with the titillation of fear and aversion makes it possible for moral scruples to be lifted, for cruelty to be enjoyed. The same thing happens in science fiction films. In the figure of the monster from outer space, the freakish, the ugly, and the predatory all converge—and provide a fantasy target for righteous bellicosity to discharge itself, and for the aesthetic enjoyment of suffering and disaster. Science fiction films are one of the purest forms of spectacle; that is, we are rarely inside anyone's feelings. (An exception is Jack Arnold's *The Incredible Shrinking Man* [1957].) We are merely spectators; we watch.

But in science fiction films, unlike horror films, there is not much horror. Suspense, shocks, surprises are mostly abjured in favor of a steady, inexorable plot. Science fiction films invite a dispassionate, aesthetic view of destruction and violence—a *technological* view. Things, objects, machinery play a major role in these films. A greater range of ethical values is embodied in the décor of these films than in the people. Things, rather than the helpless humans, are the locus of values because we experience them, rather than people, as the sources of power. According to science fiction films, man is naked without his artifacts. *They* stand for different values, they are potent, they are what get destroyed, and they are the indispensable tools for the repulse of the alien invaders or the repair of the damaged environment.

The science fiction films are strongly moralistic. The standard message is the one about the proper, or humane, use of science, versus the mad, obsessional use of science. This message the science fiction films share in common with the classic horror films of the 1930s, like *Frankenstein, The Mummy, Island of Lost Souls, Dr. Jekyll and Mr. Hyde.* (George Franju's brilliant *Les Yeux Sans Visage* [1959], called here *The Horror Chamber of Doctor Faustus,* is a more recent example.) In the horror films, we have the mad or obsessed or misguided scientist who pursues his experiments against good advice to the contrary, creates a monster or monsters, and is himself destroyed—often recognizing his folly himself, and dying in the successful effort to destroy his own creation. One science fiction equivalent of this is the scientist, usually a member of a team, who defects to the planetary invaders because "their" science is more advanced than "ours."

This is the case in *The Mysterians*, and, true to form, the renegade sees his error in the end, and from within the Mysterian space ship destroys it and himself. In *This Island Earth* (1955), the inhabitants of the beleaguered planet Metaluna propose to conquer earth, but their project is foiled by a Metalunan scientist named Exeter who, having lived on earth a while and learned to love Mozart, cannot abide such viciousness. Exeter plunges his spaceship into the ocean after returning a glamorous pair (male and female) of American physicists to earth. Metaluna dies. In *The Fly* (1958), the hero, engrossed in his basement-laboratory experiments on a matter-transmitting machine, uses himself as a subject, exchanges head and one arm with a housefly which had accidentally gotten into the machine, becomes a monster, and with his last shred of human will destroys his laboratory and orders his wife to kill him. His discovery, for the good of mankind, is lost.

Being a clearly labeled species of intellectual, scientists in science fiction films are always liable to crack up or go off the deep end. In *Conquest of Space* (1955), the scientist-commander of an international expedition to Mars suddenly acquires scruples about the blasphemy involved in the undertaking, and begins reading the Bible mid-journey instead of attending to his duties. The commander's son, who is his junior officer and always addresses his father as "General," is forced to kill the old man when he tries to prevent the ship from landing on Mars. In this film, both sides of the ambivalence toward scientists are given voice. Generally, for a scientific enterprise to be treated entirely sympathetically in these films, it needs the certificate of utility. Science, viewed without ambivalence, means an efficacious response to danger. Disinterested intellectual curiosity rarely appears in any form other than caricature, as a maniacal dementia that cuts one off from normal human relations. But this suspicion is usually directed at the scientist rather than his work. The creative scientist may become a martyr to his own discovery, through an accident or by pushing things too far. But the implication remains that other men, less imaginative—in short, technicians—could have administered the same discovery better and more safely. The most ingrained contemporary mistrust of the intellect is visited, in these movies, upon the scientist-as-intellectual.

The message that the scientist is one who releases forces which, if not controlled for good, could destroy man himself seems innocuous enough. One of the oldest images of the scientist is Shakespeare's Prospero, the overdetached scholar forcibly retired from society to a desert island, only partly in control of the magic forces in which he dabbles. Equally classic is the figure of the scientist as satanist (*Doctor Faustus*, and stories of Poe and Hawthorne). Science is magic, and man has always known that there is black magic as well as white. But it is not enough to remark that contemporary attitudes— as reflected in science fiction films—remain ambivalent, that the scientist is treated as both satanist and savior. The proportions have changed, because of the new context in which the old admiration and fear of the scientist are located. For his sphere of influence is no longer local, himself or his immediate community. It is planetary, cosmic.

One gets the feeling, particularly in the Japanese films but not only there, that a mass trauma exists over the use of nuclear weapons and the possibility of future nuclear wars. Most of the science fiction films bear witness to this trauma, and, in a way, attempt to exorcise it.

The accidental awakening of the super-destructive monster who has slept in the earth since prehistory is, often, an obvious metaphor for the Bomb. But there are many explicit references as well. In *The Mysterians*, a probe ship from the planet Mysteroid has landed on earth, near Tokyo. Nuclear warfare having been practiced on Mysteroid for centuries (their civilization is "more advanced than ours"), ninety percent of those now born on the planet have to be destroyed at birth, because of defects caused by the huge amounts of Strontium 90 in their diet. The Mysterians have come to earth to marry earth women, and possibly to take over our relatively uncontaminated planet. ... In *The Incredible Shrinking Man*, the John Doe hero is the victim of a gust of radiation which blows over the water, while he is out boating with his wife; the radiation causes him to grow smaller and smaller, until at the end of the movie he steps through the fine mesh of a window screen to become "the infinitely small." . . . In *Rodan*, a horde of monstrous carnivorous prehistoric insects, and finally a pair of giant flying reptiles (the prehistoric Archeopteryx), are hatched from dormant eggs in the depths of a mine shaft by the impact of nuclear test explosions, and go on to destroy a good part of the world before they are felled by the molten lava of a volcanic eruption. . . . In the English film, *The Day the Earth Caught Fire*, two simultaneous hydrogen bomb tests by the United States and Russia change by 11 degrees the tilt of the earth on its axis and alter the earth's orbit so that it begins to approach the sun.

Radiation casualties—ultimately, the conception of the whole world as a casualty of nuclear testing and nuclear warfare—is the most ominous of all the notions with which science fiction films deal. Universes become expendable. Worlds become contaminated, burnt out, exhausted, obsolete. In *Rocketship X-M* (1950) explorers from the earth land on Mars, where they learn that atomic warfare has destroyed Martian civilization. In George Pal's *The War of the Worlds* (1953), reddish spindly alligator-skinned creatures from Mars invade the earth because their planet is becoming too cold to be inhabitable. In *This Island Earth*, also American, the planet Metaluna, whose population has long ago been driven underground by warfare, is dying under the missile attacks of an enemy planet. Stocks of uranium, which power the force field shielding Metaluna, have been used up; and an unsuccessful expedition is sent to earth to enlist earth scientists to devise new sources for nuclear power. In Joseph Losey's *The Damned* (1961), nine icy-cold radioactive children are being reared by a fanatical scientist in a dark cave on the English coast to be the only survivors of the inevitable nuclear Armageddon.

There is a vast amount of wishful thinking in science fiction films, some of it touching, some of it depressing. Again and again, one detects the hunger for a "good war," which poses no moral problems, admits of no moral qualifications. The imagery of science fiction films will satisfy the most bellicose addict of war films, for a lot of the satisfactions of war films pass, untransformed, into science fiction films. Examples: the dogfights between earth "fighter rockets" and alien spacecraft in the *Battle of Outer Space* (1959); the escalating firepower in the successive assaults upon the invaders in *The Mysterians*, which Dan Talbot correctly described as a non-stop holocaust; the spectacular bombardment of the underground fortress of Metaluna in *This Island Earth*.

Yet at the same time the bellicosity of science fiction films is neatly channeled into the yearning for peace, or for at least peaceful coexistence. Some scientist generally takes sententious note of the fact that it took the planetary invasion to make the warring nations of the earth come to their senses and suspend their own conflicts. One of the main themes of many science fiction films—the color ones usually, because they have the budget and resources to develop the military spectacle—is this UN fantasy, a fantasy of united warfare. (The same wishful UN theme cropped up in a recent spectacular which is not science fiction, *Fifty-Five Days in Peking* [1963]. There, topically enough, the Chinese, the Boxers, play the role of Martian invaders who unite the earthmen, in this case the United States, England, Russia, France, Germany, Italy, and Japan.) A great enough disaster cancels all enmities and calls upon the utmost concentration of earth resources.

Science—technology—is conceived of as the great unifier. Thus the science fiction films also project a Utopian fantasy. In the classic models of Utopian thinking—Plato's *Republic*, Campanella's *City of the Sun*, More's *Utopia*, Swift's land of the Houyhnhnms, Voltaire's Eldorado—society had worked out a perfect consensus. In these societies reasonableness had achieved an unbreakable supremacy over the emotions. Since no disagreement or social conflict was intellectually plausible, none was possible. As in Melville's *Typee*, "they all think the same." The universal rule of reason meant universal agreement. It is interesting, too, that societies in which reason was pictured as totally ascendant were also traditionally pictured as having an ascetic or materially frugal and economically simple mode of life. But in the Utopian world community projected by science fiction films, totally pacified and ruled by scientific consensus, the demand for simplicity of material existence would be absurd.

Yet alongside the hopeful fantasy of moral simplification and international unity embodied in the science fiction films lurk the deepest anxieties about contemporary existence. I don't mean only the very real trauma of the Bomb—that it has been used, that there are enough now to kill everyone on earth many times over, that those new bombs may very well be used. Besides these new anxieties about physical disaster, the prospect of universal mutilation and even annihilation, the science fiction films reflect powerful anxieties about the condition of the individual psyche.

For science fiction films may also be described as a popular mythology for the contemporary *negative* imagination about the impersonal. The other-world creatures that seek to take "us" over are an "it," not a "they." The planetary invaders are usually zombielike. Their movements are either cool, mechanical, or lumbering, blobby. But it amounts to the same thing. If they are non-human in form, they proceed with an absolutely regular, unalterable movement (unalterable save by destruction). If they are human in form—dressed in space suits, etc.—then they obey the most rigid military discipline, and display no personal characteristics whatsoever. And it is this regime of emotionlessness, of impersonality, of regimentation, which they will impose on the earth if they are successful. "No more love, no more beauty, no more pain," boasts a converted earthling in *The Invasion of the Body Snatchers* (1956). The half-earthling, half-alien children in *The Children of the Damned* (1960) are absolutely emotionless, move as a group and understand each others' thoughts, and are all prodigious intellects. They are the wave of the future, man in his next stage of development.

These alien invaders practice a crime which is worse than murder. They do not simply kill the person. They obliterate him. In *The War of the Worlds*, the ray which issues from the rocket ship disintegrates all persons and objects in its path, leaving no trace of them but a light ash. In Honda's *The H-Man* (1959), the creeping blob melts all flesh with which it comes in contact. If the blob, which looks like a huge hunk of red Jello and can crawl across floors and up and down walls, so much as touches your bare foot, all that is left of you is a heap of clothes on the floor. (A more articulated, size-multiplying blob is the villain in the English film *The Creeping Unknown* [1956].) In another version of this fantasy, the body is preserved but the person is entirely reconstituted as the automatized servant or agent of the alien powers. This is, of course, the vampire fantasy in new dress. The person is really dead, but he doesn't know it. He is "undead," he has become an "unperson." It happens to a whole California town in *The Invasion of the Body Snatchers*, to several earth scientists in *This Island Earth*, and to assorted innocents in *It Came From Outer Space, Attack of the Puppet People* (1958), and *The Brain Eaters* (1958). As the victim always backs away from the vampire's horrifying embrace, so in science fiction films the person always fights being "taken over"; he wants to retain his humanity. But once the deed has been done, the victim is eminently satisfied with his condition. He has not been converted from human amiability to monstrous "animal" bloodlust (a meta-phoric exaggeration of sexual desire), as in the old vampire fantasy. No, he has simply become far more efficient—the very model of technocratic man, purged of emotions, volitionless, tranquil, obedi-ent to all orders. (The dark secret behind human nature used to be the upsurge of the animal—as in *King Kong*. The threat to man, his availability to dehumanization, lay in his own animality. Now the danger is understood as residing in man's ability to be turned into a machine.)

The rule, of course, is that this horrible and irremediable form of murder can strike anyone in the film except the hero. The hero and his family, while greatly threatened, always escape this fate and by the end of the film the invaders have been repulsed or destroyed. I know of only one exception, *The Day That Mars Invaded Earth* (1963), in which after all the standard struggles the scientist-hero, his wife, and their two children are "taken over" by the alien invaders—and that's that. (The last minutes of the film show them being incinerated by the Martians' rays and their ash silhouettes flushed down their empty swimming pool, while their simulacra drive off in the family car.) Another variant but upbeat switch on the rule occurs in *The Creation of the Humanoids* (1964), where the hero discovers at the end of the film that he, too, has been turned into a metal robot, complete with highly efficient and virtually indestruct-ible mechanical insides, although he didn't know it and detected no difference in himself. He learns, however, that he will shortly be upgraded into a "humanoid" having all the properties of a real man.

Of all the standard motifs of science fiction films, this theme of dehumanization is perhaps the most fascinating. For, as I have indicated, it is scarcely a black-and-white situation, as in the old vampire films. The attitude of the science fiction films toward depersonalization is mixed. On the one hand, they deplore it as the ultimate horror. On the other hand, certain characteristics of the dehumanized invaders, modulated and disguised—such as the ascendancy of reason over feelings, the idealization of teamwork and the consensus-creating activities of science, a marked degree of moral simplification—are precisely traits of the savior-scientist. It is interesting that when the scientist in these films is treated negatively, it is usually done through the portrayal of an individual scientist who holes up in his laboratory and neglects his fiancée or his loving wife and children, obsessed by his daring and dangerous experiments. The scientist as a loyal member of a team, and therefore considerably less individualized, is treated quite respectfully.

There is absolutely no social criticism, of even the most implicit kind, in science fiction films. No criticism, for example, of the conditions of our society which create the impersonality and dehumanization which science fiction fantasies displace onto the influence of an alien It. Also, the notion of science as a social activity, interlocking with social and political interests, is unacknowledged. Science is simply either adventure (for good or evil) or a technical response to danger. And, typically, when the fear of science is paramount—when science is conceived of as black magic rather than white—the evil has no attribution beyond that of the perverse will of an individual scientist. In science fiction films the antithesis of black magic and white is drawn as a split between technology, which is beneficent, and the errant individual will of a lone intellectual.

Thus, science fiction films can be looked at as thematically central allegory, replete with standard modern attitudes. The theme of depersonalization (being "taken over") which I have been talking about is a new allegory reflecting the age-old awareness of man that, sane, he is always perilously close to insanity and unreason. But there is something more here than just a recent, popular image which expresses man's perennial, but largely unconscious, anxiety about his sanity. The image derives most of its power from a supplementary and historical anxiety, also not experienced *consciously* by most people, about the depersonalizing conditions of modern urban life. Similarly, it is not enough to note that science fiction allegories are one of the new myths about—that is, one of the ways of accommodating to and negating—the perennial human anxiety about death. (Myths of heaven and hell, and of ghosts, had the same function.) For, again, there is a historically specifiable twist which intensifies the anxiety. I mean, the trauma suffered by everyone in the middle of the 20th century when it became clear that, from now on to the end of human history, every person would spend his individual life under the threat not only of individual death, which is certain, but of something almost insupportable psychologically—collective incineration and extinction which could come at any time, virtually without warning.

From a psychological point of view, the imagination of disaster does not greatly differ from one period in history to another. But from a political and moral point of view, it does. The expectation of the apocalypse may be the occasion for a radical disaffiliation from society, as when thousands of Eastern European Jews in the 17th century, hearing that Sabbatai Zevi had been proclaimed the Messiah and that the end of the world was imminent, gave up their homes and businesses and began the trek to Palestine. But people take the news of their doom in diverse ways. It is reported that in 1945 the populace of Berlin received without great agitation the news that Hitler had decided to kill them all, before the Allies arrived, because they had not been worthy enough to win the war. We are, alas, more in the position of the Berliners of 1945 than of the Jews of 17th century Eastern Europe; and our response is closer to theirs, too. What I am suggesting is that the imagery of disaster in science fiction is above all the emblem of an *inadequate response*. I don't mean to bear down on the films for this. They themselves are only a sampling, stripped of sophistication, of the inadequacy of most people's response to the unassimilable terrors that infect their consciousness. The interest of the films, aside from their considerable amount of cinematic charm, consists in this intersection between a naïve and largely debased commercial art product and the most profound dilemmas of the contemporary situation.

Ours is indeed an age of extremity. For we live under continual threat of two equally fearful, but seemingly opposed, destinies: unremitting banality and inconceivable terror. It is fantasy, served out in large rations by the popular arts, which allows most people to cope with these twin specters. For one job that fantasy can do is to lift us out of the unbearably humdrum and to distract us from terrors—real or anticipated—by an escape into exotic, dangerous situations which have last-minute happy endings. But another of the things that fantasy can do is to normalize what is psychologically unbearable, thereby inuring us to it. In one case, fantasy beautifies the world. In the other, it neutralizes it.

The fantasy in science fiction films does both jobs. The films reflect world-wide anxieties, and they serve to allay them. They inculcate a strange apathy concerning the processes of radiation, contamination, and destruction which I for one find haunting and depressing. The naïve level of the films neatly tempers the sense of otherness, of alien-ness, with the grossly familiar. In particular, the dialogue of most science fiction films, which is of a monumental but often touching banality, makes them wonderfully, unintentionally funny. Lines like "Come quickly, there's a monster in my bathtub," "We must do something about this," "Wait, Professor. There's someone on the telephone," "But that's incredible," and the old American stand-by, "I hope it works!" are hilarious in the context of picturesque and deafening holocaust. Yet the films also contain something that is painful and in deadly earnest.

There is a sense in which all these movies are in complicity with the abhorrent. They neutralize it, as I have said. It is no more, perhaps, than the way all art draws its audience into a circle of complicity with the thing represented. But in these films we have to do with things which are (quite literally) unthinkable. Here, "thinking about the unthinkable"—not in the way of Herman Kahn, as a subject for calculation, but as a subject for fantasy—becomes, however inadvertently, itself a somewhat questionable act from a moral point of view. The films perpetuate clichés about identity, volition, power, knowledge, happiness, social consensus, guilt, responsibility which are, to say the least, not serviceable in our present extremity. But collective nightmares cannot be banished by demonstrating that they are, intellectually and morally, fallacious. This nightmare—the one reflected, in various registers, in the science fiction films—is too close to our reality.

How to Play Utopia: Some Brief
Notes on the Distinctiveness
of Utopian Fiction

by Michael Holquist

"God alone is worthy of supreme seriousness, but man is made God's plaything, and that is the best part of him. Therefore every man and woman should live life accordingly, and play the noblest games, and be of another mind from what they are at present ..." —Plato, *Laws*

Roger Caillois has written that "for a long time the study of games was hardly more than a history of toys. Particular attention was paid to the tools or accessories of games rather than to the games themselves—their characteristics, their laws, the instincts they presuppose, the kind of satisfaction they procure." [1] Many *histories* of games can be so dismissed.[2] But *legends* about the *origins* of certain games can sometimes reveal precisely those qualities which Caillois seeks. Take, for example, the Chinese legend concerning the invention of chess:

> Three hundred and seventy-nine years after the time of Confucius, Hung-Ko-Chu, king of Kiang-Nan, sent an expedition into Shen-Si under the command of Han-Sing. After a successful campaign the soldiers were put into winter quarters, where they became impatient and demanded to be sent home. Han-Sing realized the urgent necessity of calming them if he was to finish his operations in the

"How to Play Utopia" by Michael Holquist. From *Yale French Studies*, XLI (1968), pp. 106–23. Reprinted by permission of *Yale French Studies*.

[1] "Unity of Play: Diversity of Games," *Diogenes*, no. 19 (Fall, 1957), p. 93.

[2] For a classic example of such history, see H. J. R. Murray, *A History of Board Games Other Than Chess* (Oxford, 1952).

following year; he was a man of genius as well as a good soldier, and after considerable contemplation he invented the game of chess which would serve as an amusement in times of leisure and, being founded on the principles of war, would excite their military ardor. The stratagem fulfilled his expectations; the soldiers were delighted and in their daily contests forgot the inconveniences of their position. In the spring the general took the field again and in a few months added the rich Shen-Si territory to the kingdom of Kiang-Nan.

Chinese Annals.[3]

This legend has essentially the same pattern as is found in the Persian, Indian, and Japanese legends, a pattern in which the game is invented as a *substitute for battle*. Inherent in this process of substitution are the characteristics, laws, presupposed instincts, and the nature of satisfaction which are involved in the game of chess, in many respects the game of games. In what follows I shall speak in more detail about these implications in chess in order to develop an analogy with the structure of utopian fiction. Baldly stated, my thesis is that the relationship of chess to battle is roughly parallel to the relationship which obtains between utopia and actual society.

The most obvious thing about the relationship of chess to battle is that the game is an abstraction, a highly stylized mode of combat. "Inside the play-ground an absolute and peculiar order reigns ... [play] creates order, *is* order. Into an imperfect world and into the confusion of life it brings a temporary, a limited perfection. Play demands order absolute and supreme." [4] There is no more graphic an image of confusion than a real battle (one thinks of Stendhal, or Tolstoy—or the latest dispatches from Viet Nam). There is no more graphic an image of order than the game of chess (one thinks, perhaps, of the almost god-like perfection of such encounters as the 1892 match game in Havana between Steinitz and Tchigorin). It is not without significance that the first "computer" (although it was a hoax) was designed to play chess,[5] or that a favorite pastime of computer programmers today is to play chess with their machines. By perceiving the particular dynamic and degree of stylization which rules in chess, the order of the game can be reconciled with the chaos of battle. This stylization is grounded in borders, or

---

[3] Quoted in: R. N. Coles, *The Chess-Player's Weekend Book* (London, 1950), p. 54.

[4] Johan Huizinga, *Homo Ludens* (Boston, 1964), p. 10.

[5] The reference here is, of course, to the von Kempelen robot of 1770.

exclusions. These are defined by rules, which determine furniture, time, place, and object.

What characterizes the rules of chess is their inflexibility. If you break the rules, you cease to do chess. War has its rules, sometimes rigidly codified, as in the chivalric code, or the Geneva Convention, but they can be broken by parties who thereby do not cease to be at war. It is literally true that "all is fair in love and war."

The furniture consists in the board and pieces. The relationship to battlefield and opposing armies is clear enough in these, and their history, not to require further comment. Except perhaps to stress the closeness of the relationship between various types of pieces and the society in which they are employed. Most games in the West are now played with figures of the Staunton design, which bear only the most tenuous and sketchily iconic relationship to actual figures. If chess were rhetoric, the Staunton king, for instance, would be called a synecdoche. But in the past, and as we shall see, even now, in some striking instances, the pieces have reflected their historical hour in much greater particularity: the bishops have been carved in full regalia, the king, queen, knights, and pawns have been modelled on the particular rulers and warriors of the place and time in which the set was made. In short, they owe their design more to the social hierarchy than to the technology of their actual manufacture. The Staunton set is, on the other hand, born of the lathe. The close relationship of sets in the past to actual costumes and politics has important implications which we shall refer to later. At this point what is important to note is the process by which vast armies are reduced to 32 pieces, the blind movements of troops to the inflexible symmetry of the permissible moves, all of which is accomplished on 64 perfect squares.

So much has been written on the peculiar time and place of games, that it is unnecessary to rehearse the arguments here.[6] In order to proceed it will suffice to remember that the time and place are set outside the everyday rhythms of experience, and as such are free from the contingency which haunts actual engagements of

[6] Caillois and Huizinga are good on this, but possibly the most succinct statement of the peculiar time and space of games is to be found in: Friedrich Georg Jünger, *Die Spiele: ein Schlussel zu ihrer Bedeutung* (Frankfurt am Main, 1953), pp. 91–97. Hans-Georg Gadamer is also very suggestive on this topic in: *Wahrheit und Methode* (Tübingen, 1965), pp. 97–105.

armies. What has been said of the arbitrariness of the game's space and time applies also to its object: to place the opposing king into that situation in which he must be captured. Checkmate is the more neutral way of describing this, but the stylized parallel with the defeat of an actual ruler or general should not be forgotten.

Now that these elementary considerations have been established, I would like to suggest some parallels between, first, chess and utopia, and then between utopia and society.

In book II of More's *Utopia*, Hythloday describes the games of the Utopians. The one he dwells on longest "is a game in which the vices fight a pitched battle with the virtues. In the latter is exhibited very cleverly, to begin with, both the strife of the vices with one another and their concerted opposition to the virtues; then, what vices are opposed to what virtues, by what forces they assail them openly, by what stratagems they attack them indirectly, by what safeguards the virtues check the power of the vices, by what arts they frustrate their designs, and finally, by what means the one side gains the victory." [7] This is not only a game in *Utopia*. It is the game *of* utopia. What More is here describing suggests the underlying structure of almost all utopian fiction. What Caillois is seeking for in a true description of particular games, may serve also as the criteria of what one looks for in the description of genres: "their characteristics, their laws, the instincts they presuppose, the kind of satisfaction they procure." In connection with utopian literature it may be said that these questions are best answered by first perceiving that each given piece of utopianism is a kind of game, or at least shares many revealing characteristics with games. This can be seen by the confrontation of parallels in a typical game—chess, with those in a typical utopia—More's.

Utopia has in common with chess first of all the general characteristic that it is a simplification, a radical stylization of something which in experience is of enormous complexity, often lacking any apparent symmetry. Chess substitutes for war, utopia for society. In each case what was rough is made smooth, what was chaotic is made orderly. The chess game has *rules*, the utopia *laws*. The chess game has its distinctive furniture, derived from battle.

[7] Sir Thomas More, *Utopia*, ed. Edward Surtz, S. J. (New Haven, Conn., 1964), p. 71.

Utopia has its characteristic counters, derived from society. Instead of knights and bishops, the utopia deploys more complex units. This is because that which chess reflects in game is in itself more comprehensible, less total than that which utopia mirrors in play. The most involved battle will engage a smaller amount of a given culture's affects than the simplest social hierarchy will of its culture. This can easily be seen by recognizing that war is only one aspect of something larger—namely, in this case, society. Since utopia strives to reflect the more complex entity of the two, its furniture must be correspondingly more numerous and diffuse. It must find counters not only for rulers and warriors, but also for farmers, lawyers, philosophers, etc. Most utopias contain these elements, but they are all reduced to manageable essentials. When critics complain that there are no great utopias they usually mean that there are no utopian novels which contain plots or characters of the depth and complexity found in more conventional works of fiction. This is to miss the point completely, to complain that chess is inferior because it lacks the body contact of football. What such critics ask for is a game with different presuppositions and satisfactions. The intention of the utopist is the polar opposite of the conventional novelist. The former intends the typical, the stylized, the manageable. The difficulties at the heart of, say, a psychological novel are precisely those which the utopist seeks to avoid. People, like everything else in utopia, must be shriven of their idiosyncrasies, must be transformed into units that can be manipulated according to a restricted set of laws and presuppositions. In utopia, surprise is a heresy. When literary critics dismiss as "mere pawns" the characters in utopian fiction, they simply valorize an objective fact.

Utopia, like chess, has its own time and place, which are set over against the world of experience. Just as chess is separated from life by its conventions, utopia cuts itself off from life by conventions of its own. These conventions vary from work to work, but there are certain frequently recurring techniques of border creation, two of which are especially defining: setting the imaginary society in a distant time or place, or both. I shall return in a moment to these methods, but in connection with More one further possibility for marking the boundaries should be mentioned. The *Utopia* bristles with name inversions, or what might be called private nouns. These names deprive what they purport to describe of the very quality which is their essence. There is the name of the place itself, somewhere which is nowhere. The Achoreans, a people without a place; Anydrus is a river without water; and Ademus is a leader with no people to lead. Samuel Butler's *Erewhon* is in the same tradition, and the play on digits, vowels, and consonants in Zamyatin's *We* is a further change rung on this tendency. This is simply one more example of the generally playful quality to be found in even the grimmest utopian literature.

More commonly utopian literature has insisted on its fictionality by setting up temporal or spatial borders between itself and actual experience. The space of utopia, the board on which the game is played, has more often than not been a continent or island, what Hans Freyer has "the political island." [8] This is as true of Plato's Atlantis as it is of More's Utopia or Diderot's "Tahiti." More recently distant planets have become the geographical locus for such speculation.

The conventional time of utopia is a more complex boundary. The time in which the fiction is set may be past, present, or future relative to the date of composition. Golden Ages are set in the past; More's utopia exists contemporaneously with More's England; *Looking Backward* and most anti-utopias are set in the future. What is distinctive about all these utopian times, however, is their subsuming quality of arbitrariness. Utopian time is more utterly a convention than is even our artificial clock time. Thus it is in a sense misleading to speak of past, present, and future in utopia. If we conceive of utopian time as a single entity, its distinguishing feature becomes more readily apparent: it exists only as an enabling device for a certain kind of speculation. W. H. Auden has written somewhere that opera is the sustained expression of those moments in life when we say "I felt like singing." By analogy, we may say that utopia is the extension of those moments when we say "What if ..." Utopias are the literature of the subjunctive mood. More often than not set in a putative future, they reverse, however, the artificial time of the grammatical subjunctive which, in most European languages, is some form of the past. But of course the past when used in this way does not refer to a temporal past. The "reference is to present or undefined time, or more truly, not to time at all (and

---

[8] *Die Politische Insel* (Berlin, 1936).

especially not to a particular past time) but to utopia, the realm of non-fact." [9] Time in utopia is deployed in much the same way, not as real time, or even as literary time, but as a convention of its own for articulating conditional possibilities. It is hypothetical or heuristic time. It is a time marked off from clock time just as surely as the time of a chess game.[10]

We have been speaking of the various ways in which utopia is hedged off from actual experience. But in so doing we have also established some of those conditions which set utopias off from other fiction on the one hand, and political programs on the other. Before proceeding further these distinctions should be made more specific. In discussing the analogies between game and utopia listed above, the objection has frequently and sometimes disconcertingly been raised that there is a sense in which all fiction has its own rules, its own time, space, etc. This objection first of all fails to take into account the *specific* quality of these attributes as they are present in utopian fiction. In the above paragraphs I have attempted to show in what this specificity consists. Beyond this, it is necessary to add that a further distinction between the worlds of conventional and utopian fiction is the completeness with which the utopia strives to describe the various necessary societal functions and institutions. Society in, say, *Anna Karenina*, or better, *La Comédie Humaine* is richly and broadly present. But while most utopias are infinitely less replete with small details, the better of them will, no matter how sketchily, at least allude to a wider range of societal institutions. The reason for this lies in the utopian impulse, which can be said to have its source in a distinctive anthropology. The utopist, before he writes a line, begins by postulating what the best man would be; he then proceeds to articulate those conditions which would best insure the rise and the continued existence of such a man. His anthropology, leads necessarily to ecology, the ecology of perfection. Thus the utopist strives to describe that world which is most conducive to nurturing the values which define the ideal man he posits. Just as no battle, no matter how strategically sound, is ever as neat as a

[9] H. W. Fowler, "Subjunctives," *A Dictionary of Modern English Usage* (Oxford, 1965).

[10] It should not be necessary to point out that the clocks used to time match games derive from the exigencies of this particular kind of competition and *not* from something inherent in *the game of chess itself.*

chess game, so is no society as coherent as utopia. Just as all the moves and elements of the chess game are directed toward one end, so are the plot and institutions of a utopian fiction aimed at the one goal—the writer's ideal man. This impulse has several consequences. Two of these reflect back on the differences between utopian and more conventional literature. One, society ceases to be a live organism in the utopia. It becomes rather a machine for manufacturing that type of man which the author sees as the best man. Two, it follows from this that if utopian characters are robots stamped out by the mold of utopian society, the relationship between the two is of a fixed, determined kind. Balzac's rooming houses and counting houses, indeed his France, have a certain completeness, but lack the coherence which is available only to the static society of utopia. This society is by definition perfect, so that any changes in it can result only in a falling away, a decline. Thus innovation is a crime in utopia, a sin against perfection. It is the organic, the shifting quality of Tolstoy's or Balzac's world which permits their characters the complexity of individual beings, part of, but not defined by, their society. By speaking of ecology in utopia one seeks to underline the fact that in the perfect state, man *is* his environment. Thus the aesthetics of the novel are wrongly applied to utopias. It is not inferior to conventional fiction, it is different from it. Another consequence is that the distinctions between various utopias can be explained as being basically the result of conflicting anthropologies. But more significantly, this view of what utopia does dramatizes somewhat more effectively than other conceptions the fact that utopian fiction is just what More suggests in his game alluded to above: the play of what a given utopist calls virtues against what he feels to be vices. It is in this quality of opposition, and the extended shape the dialectic assumes in utopias, that the difference between them and other types of social programs is to be found. The utopia dramatizes, suggests, the manifesto dictates. There are other, even more fundamental, differences, and these shall be dealt with in the conclusion.

At this point it is necessary to delve further into the emblematic or allegorical possibilities inherent in utopias. One of the consequences of the order which reigns in utopia is its pervasive sense of logic. But the logic is of a particular, contrapuntal sort. It advances by means of contrasts, the constantly shifting poles of which create a pattern of superior versus inferior men and institutions. For instance, in Thomas More there are several explicit comparisons between utopia and Europe, and several comparisons between utopia and other imaginary nations which surround it. The *Republic* is one vast fabric of such comparisons between the various stages of Plato's model community, as well as between them and Greek society. A striking example of this compulsion to contrast is found in Voltaire's *Zadig*, where in chapter XII an Egyptian, an Indian, a Chinese, a Celt, a Greek, etc. come together for dinner, and the whole action consists of a satirical confrontation of their various religious prejudices. The list could be extended, but such a course is no doubt unnecessary. The truth that each utopia exists as a value system to challenge other such systems is self-evident. In the case of most utopian fictions the tension is between the world outside the work, and the world it encloses, thus the contrast is often implicit. But in some examples, such as those just cited, and in all anti-utopias, the conflicting systems are contained in the fictions themselves. *1984*, for instance, is almost completely analogous to the game Thomas More describes: the tale it tells is made from the attempts of the virtuous rebels to overcome the stratagems of the Thought Police vices.

Now it will probably already have occurred to the reader that this allegorical quality of utopia seems to fly in the face of remarks made earlier concerning the separateness of utopia from actual experience. A game is pure, allegory is impure. But it is also true that games are played by people, who only indirectly and ambiguously share in the perfect order of their games. It is at just this point of the seeming most irreconcilable conflict between the nature of chess and utopia that a further analogy between the two will most aid us. Before going on, two more facts about chess should be remembered. The first is that in medieval Europe there existed an important body of literature referred to now as chess moralities. "It will be a matter for no surprise to anyone familiar with characteristics of the European literature of the Middle Ages to discover that works were written in which attempts were made to give a symbolical or allegorical explanation of the game of chess, or to find parallels between the organization of human life and activities and the different names and powers of the chessmen...." [11] One of these moralities was traditionally associated with Pope Innocent III, and they are also to be found in the pages of the widely read *Gesta Romanorum*. Murray, in the definitive history of the game in English, devotes thirty-four closely packed pages to the subject. The second fact which should be remembered I have hinted at earlier: the intention of medieval schoolmen who used chess for allegory did not confine itself to literature, but was reflected in the design for the pieces of some sets: "When Caxton printed the second book in English, 'The Game and Playe of the Chesse,' a translation of Cessolis, he gave a long description of each piece and pawn, and the good or bad qualities denoted by the attributes of the chessman." [12] At least one such set survives,[13] together with another morality set, even more explicit, representing the forces of good and evil (Crusaders and Moslems, Angels and Devils).[14] Thus the Manichean game Thomas More describes is no mere invention.

But, it will be said, utopias show not simply the conflict of abstract virtues and vices, such as Gluttony and Abstinence, Pride and Modesty, which is the case in chess moralities. Utopias deal with much more concrete tensions, problems that bear a much closer relationship to specific historical conflicts between various economic, legal, religious systems, etc. But the same tendency is also to be observed in the history of chess, [where we frequently find sets which exemplify] the urge to read specific values into the tempting white and black possibilities of the chessmen. [Certain Soviet sets, for example, attempt] to turn the battle setting of chess into a model of class warfare. The vices are specifically identified here as excessive wealth in the "queen," as household troops of the Czar's life guard in the "bishops," and the pawns are chained laborers. The virtuous "queen" is a farm woman in native costume, and the "bishops" are Red Army cavalrymen. The list of attempts to reflect even more specific situations, such as actual battles, could be extended indefinitely: there exist sets modelled on the American Civil War; Clovis vs. Alaric, Napoleon's Egyptian campaign (at

[11] H. J. R. Murray, *A History of Chess* (Oxford, 1913), p. 529.
[12] Donald M. Liddell, et al., *Chessman* (New York, 1937), p. 19.
[13] See p. 23 of Liddell's book.
[14] Illustrated on p. 82 in Liddell.

least eleven of these sets are known); Gustavus Adolphus vs. Ferdinand of Austria; Napoleon vs. Francis I of Austria; Napoleon vs. Frederick the Great; Waterloo; Saratoga; there is even a set with British soldiers opposing Zulus! A logical extension of this impulse is to leave the strictures of chess behind in order more completely to capture the details of the battle represented in the play itself. This has in fact been done, as in the case of the chess-like game invented by François Gilot in 1855, modelled on the taking of Sevastopol during the Crimean War, and the "strategy" games popular among college students are a current manifestation of the same impulse: "Stalingrad," "Gettysburg," etc.

In both sets of examples listed above, those concerning chess moralities and those concerning sets designed to mirror historical battles, there is a common denominator to be observed. In each case men have attempted to make the abstract model of combat which is the game into a set of specific oppositions. More, they have sought to give value to that which is in its essence without value. The fact that one "king" is a piece modelled after Napoleon and the other is represented by a figure modelled on the Duke of Wellington does not affect the nature of the chess contest itself. In such a game Napoleon is just as likely to "win" the stylized battle of Waterloo as Wellington. The game itself is a kind of *langue;* such historically based chess sets are simply an attempt to make more particular the *parole* of the contest in games that are actually played. The model of battle in chess is, however, so pure that it can be filled out in an actual instance with *any* values without the real nature of the game being in any way affected. What is important to note, however, is that when chess is played with such figures, the game may be said no longer to be a stylization of just any battle, but given the specific furniture with which it is played, a stylization of the battle of Waterloo, Saratoga, Gettysburg, etc. By so reducing the historical battle, the issue that was there decided in life, becomes an open possibility again in the game. In the model is the freedom which only play gives, and the stylized battle of Waterloo may have a different outcome each time the game is played.

In utopias an analogous dynamic can be perceived. In the study of utopias it is a commonplace that there exists a bond between the imaginary land presented in a given fiction, and the actual society in which it was written. "Swift, Voltaire, and even Diderot set their satirical novels in a 'never and nowhere' which nevertheless faithfully reflects the essential characteristics of contemporary England and France." [15] This relationship will, of course, be much closer in satirical utopias than in less specifically oriented examples of the genre, but, even in More's Utopia we have the word of Erasmus that More "represented chiefly Britain." [16] What the nature of the relationship between a utopia, and the actual society from which it springs, truly is, should now be clear. It is, to a greater or lesser extent, the same as that which obtains between the concrete representations of historical figures in the chessmen and the abstract structure of the game itself. Thus the geography of More's imaginary land in its insular configuration, in its architectural details (a bridge much like Tower Bridge, etc.), is similar to the actualities of England, much as the Napoleon, Wellington, and other pieces in the set alluded to above are similar to actualities of the Battle of Waterloo. But just as these figures are subsumed by a set of laws peculiar to chess when a game is played using them, so do the projected artifacts from English reality become subordinated to the rules of More's utopia. The complex social, economic, and religious factors which are in the grip of the course of English history in reality, when reduced and stylized into counters, become accessible to the freedom of play in the utopia. The irreversibility of history is stemmed, and outcomes determined by the contingency of actual experience, can, in utopia, be reversed in the freedom of the utopist's imagination. Another set of laws obtains in the utopia, arbitrary but infinitely open to recombination. Utopia is play with ideas.

There will be those who say, "But a chess game is free in a way that utopias are not. Even if one takes into account the limitless combinations available to the utopist *before* he describes his imaginary society, once he has done so, the shape of that society is fixed, it cannot be 'played' again in the way chess may be replayed." This objection may be answered by pointing out that not only does the author of utopias play the game, so does the *reader* of utopias. And the best examples of the genre are arranged in such a

[15] Georg Lukacs, *The Historical Novel*, tr. H. and S. Michell (Boston, 1963), p. 20.
[16] *Opus epistolarum Des. Erasmi Roterodami*, ed. P. S. Allen et al. (12 vols., Oxford, 1906–58), vol. 4, p. 21.

way that they may be "played" again as often as they are read. That is, most utopias have open endings. After the struggle of vices and virtues has been described, the utopist leaves it up to the reader to decide who lost, who won. Two examples of such endings should make the point. After Hythloday has concluded his description of Utopia, Thomas More, or rather the counter in the book which bears this name, says, "Meanwhile, though in other respects he is a man of the most undoubted learning as well as of the greatest knowledge of human affairs, I cannot agree with all that he said. But I readily admit that there are very many features in the Utopian Commonwealth which it is easier for me to wish for in our countries than to have any hope of seeing realized." These are the last words in the book, especially fitting in one that has as its subtitle "A Truely Golden Handbook, No less Beneficial than Entertaining." For that is precisely what More has done—given the reader ideas to *entertain*. The conclusion of Diderot's *Supplement to Bougainville's Voyage* has the same open quality. After reading and discussing the putative notes of a chaplain who accompanied the French admiral to Tahiti, and in which a rather golden image of those islands is given, B says, "Let us follow the good chaplain's example—be monks in France and savages in Tahiti." To which A replies, "Put on the costume of the country you visit, but keep the suit of clothes you will need to go home in." This statement goes a long way toward explaining the pattern, so often remarked in utopias, of voyage and return. Hythloday goes to utopia, but he comes back to Holland. Diderot's chaplain goes to Tahiti, but returns to France. After symbolically dwelling for so long in the city Socrates spins out of words in the *Republic*, the listeners are brought back to their villa. In so doing, the returned voyagers leave open the contrast between the two worlds between which they shuttle, and it is the reader who, having observed "the vices fight a pitched battle with the virtues," as More says, decides "by what means the one side gains the victory."

A game is, as we have seen, something set off, the borders between what is, and what is not the game are always clear, and when they are violated the play ceases. But there are those who have forgotten that utopia is a game, and in transgressing the limits of what marks it off as play, have wrought great harm to themselves and others. They have attempted in the world of experience what is possible only in the freedom of the second world. One such is Etienne Cabet, who in 1840 published his Socialist utopia *Voyage en Icarie.* Not content with his imagined society, Cabet in 1848-9 attempted to found an actual community based on the principles of his book. What ensued is a history of disasters, and Cabet died a broken man in St. Louis, Missouri seven years later. Other examples abound, but in each case the attempt to translate a society enacted in the mind into praxis (a community in Texas or California) has ended in chaos. The reason, in each case, is the same: just as you cannot order real battles according to the logic of chess, so you cannot erect actual communities based on the logic of utopia. Not recognizing the bounds between stylized game and causal reality is to do violence to the complexity of existence. "The function of play in the higher forms ... can largely be derived from the two basic aspects under which we meet it: as a contest *for* something or a representation *of* something. These two functions can unite in such a way that the game represents a contest, or else becomes a contest, for the best representation of something." [17] Thus, in the game of utopia, men may be reduced to pawns for the sake of a better representation; to attempt the same reduction in life leads to the police state. It is important to know how to *play* utopia.

I have stressed throughout certain parallels between chess and utopia. In order to forestall the objection that this is a baroque exercise, or a further twist on chess moralities, let me hasten to add that in doing so one has not lost his sense of the enormous disparities between the two arms of the analogy. One might best accede to the objection by simply pointing out that chess and utopia are both a form of *play,* but different kinds of *games.* In this paper I have attempted to show only the similarities between the two, believing the differences to be obvious enough not to require comment. Beyond, that is, pointing out the obvious fact that chess is much less complex, much less affective and more purely a game, than utopia. But it is in just this quality of the utopia's greater complexity, and, one might add, seriousness, that its power to move us lies.

Before leaving the subject, one more parallel between chess and utopia must be mentioned. In speaking of the two as we have, the desire throughout has been to answer the questions from Caillois

[17] Huizinga, p. 13.

with which we began. Thus my remarks have been addressed, in connection with both, to "their characteristics, their laws, the instincts they pre-suppose"; it is time now to consider "the kind of satisfaction they procure." In order to do this we must be aware that each has a double object, one which satisfies the requirements of the game itself, and one which satisfies the players. The object of the game of chess is different from the game of utopia, but the reason why people play both is the same. The object of the game of chess is to checkmate one's opponent. The object of the game of utopia is to show why one set of social virtues, worked out in comprehensive institutions, is superior to others. In this they differ. But there is an end the player of each has which transcends that of the game itself. The player's end is to achieve a particular kind of freedom. What Harry Berger has written about the "Green World" of Renaissance literature will serve as a partial evocation of what this freedom is: it is to revel in a second world, "the playground, laboratory, theater, or battlefield of the mind, a model or construct which the mind creates, a time or place which it clears in order to withdraw from the actual world ... separating itself from the casual and confused region of everyday existence, it promises a clarified image of the world it replaces." [18]

Speculation about utopia is more important now than it ever was. We have recently all too often forgotten, and to our sorrow, that perfection is a game, something available to the mind, but not to the state. When we have stopped playing, when we have attempted to instrument the seductive but inhuman logic of games in actual programs, the consequence has inevitably been pogroms. Thus, utopia perceived as game is a kind of speculative instrument. In the codifiable laws of utopia so understood, we may speculate on the unchartable laws of history. We may even bear off that palm, arrive at that time which Plato invokes in the last lines of his *Republic*, when "we shall be at peace with Heaven and with ourselves, both during our sojourn here and when, like victors in the Games collecting gifts from their friends, we receive the prize of justice; and so, not here only, but in the journey of a thousand years of which I have told you, we shall fare well."

[18] "The Renaissance Imagination: Second World and Green World," *Centennial Review*, vol. IX, no. 1 (Winter, 1965), p. 46.

The Apocalyptic Imagination, Science Fiction, and American Literature

by David Ketterer

I

If, at its most exalted level, apocalyptic literature is religious, the concerns of such a literature, at its most popular level, find expression in the gothic mode and especially in science fiction. Clearly, the introduction of the other, the *outré*, whether in terms of supernatural manifestations or creatures from outer space, is going to upset man's conception of his own situation and prompt him to relate his existence to a broader framework. It is the particular function of all worthwhile science fiction to explore the philosophical consequences of any such radical disorientation.

The apocalyptic imagination, I submit, finds its purest outlet in science fiction. And in so far as science fiction concerns itself with the "sense of an ending," Kermode's understanding of the apocalyptic impulse acquires a new relevance.[1] Indeed while W. H.

[1] The title of Stephen and Lois Rose's book *The Shattered Ring: Science Fiction and the Quest for Meaning* (Richmond, Va., 1970), but nothing else about it, is suggestive here. More suggestive is a footnote R. W. B. Lewis includes in *Trials of the Word*: "The huge contribution of science fiction ... to modern apocalyptic literature would be very much worth investigating ..." (p. 193).

Auden talks about detective fiction in terms of the "phantasy of being returned to the Garden of Eden," Leslie Fiedler adduces that the dream of apocalypse is the myth of science fiction, "the myth of the end of man, of the transcendence or transformation of the human—a vision quite different from that of the extinction of our species by the Bomb, which seems stereotype rather than archetype. ..." [2] When Frye speaks of "the Flood archetype," the cosmic disaster, as characteristic of science fiction, he is insufficiently sensitive to the subsequent transformation.[3]

For the reader, an apocalyptic transformation results from the creation of a new condition, based upon a process of extrapolation and analogy, whereby man's horizons—temporal, spatial, scientific, and ultimately philosophic—are abruptly expanded. Science-fiction stories may be roughly grouped into three categories, depending upon the basis of the extrapolation involved. A writer may extrapolate the future consequences of present circumstances, in which case he will probably produce sociological science fiction within the "utopia"/dystopia range.[4] Secondly, and this is a frequently related category, typified by much of H. G. Wells' work, he may extrapolate the consequences following the modification of an existent condition.[5] This modification, as Kingsley Amis notes, frequently takes the form "of some innovation in science or pseudo-science or pseudo-technology" or "some change or disturb-

[2] W. H. Auden, "The Guilty Vicarage," *Harper's Magazine*, CXCVI (May 1948), p. 412. Leslie A. Fiedler, "The New Mutants," *Partisan Review*, XXXII (fall 1965), p. 508.

[3] *Anatomy of Criticism*, p. 203. It is, of course, true that a good many science-fictional ideas derive, however unconsciously, from a rationalistic appropriation of archetypes in the Book of Revelation. For example, the image of an insect with a human head, which figures in the film *The Fly*, has some affinity with the apocalyptic plague of locusts with human faces. Certainly the various monsters that science-fiction films have envisaged as devastating the globe are generically connected with the beasts of the Apocalypse.

[4] See, for example, John Brunner's Hugo-award winner *Stand on Zanzibar* (New York, 1969), in which one of the protagonists, Donald Hogan, prior to his very literal transformation, finds himself "suspended between the wreck of former convictions and the solidification of new ones ..." (p. 198).

[5] See, for example, Fritz Leiber's *The Wanderer* (New York, 1964), which details the consequences when a new planet comes literally within human ken....

ance or local anomaly in physical conditions." [6] Thirdly, the most philosophically oriented science fiction, extrapolating on what we know in the context of our vaster ignorance, comes up with a startling *donnée*, or rationale, that puts humanity in a radically new perspective. In the second and third categories, the element of analogy becomes increasingly evident. Needless to say, the three categories overlap, and distinction depends upon emphasis.

In spite of an over-all emphasis on ideas in science fiction, the author's extrapolative structures rarely lend themselves to overt allegorical ends, because of the danger of jeopardizing the illusion of a surface verisimilitude.[7] What all science fiction aims at is destroying old assumptions and suggesting a new, and often visionary, reality. The extent to which science fiction is satiric is particularly apparent in the dystopias treated by Mark R. Hillegas.[8] As for the other side of the coin, Samuel R. Delany writes:

> The vision ... that sf tries for seems to me very close to the vision of poetry, particularly poetry as it concerned the nineteenth century Symbolists. No matter how disciplined its creation, to move into an unreal world demands a brush with mysticism. Virtually all the classics of speculative fiction are mystical.[9]

But the mysticism must never exceed the bounds of plausibility, or

[6] *New Maps of Hell* (New York, 1960), pp. 18, 24. The effect of science is pre-eminent. J. O. Bailey, in *Pilgrims Through Space and Time: Trends and Patterns in Scientific and Utopian Fiction* (New York, 1947), notes, ". . . the First Men of Stapledon's *Last and First Men* (London, 1930) think of science as a religion, not merely because 'it was through science that men had gained some insight into the nature of the physical world, but rather because the application of scientific principles had revolutionized their material circumstance'" (p. 296).

[7] C. S. Lewis' allegorical trilogy *Out of the Silent Planet, Voyage to Venus, That Hideous Strength* (London, 1938, 1943, 1946), is a mix of fantasy and science fiction.

[8] *The Future as Nightmare: H. G. Wells and the Anti-Utopians* (New York, 1967), *passim*. In so far as academic criticism has grappled with an understanding of science fiction as a genre, the tendency has been to consider its satiric aspects. See Robert M. Philmus, *Into the Unknown: The Evolution of Science Fiction from Godwin to H. G. Wells* (Berkeley and Los Angeles, 1970), for a recent example.

[9] "About Five Thousand One Hundred and Seventy-Five Words," *Extrapolation: A Science Fiction Newsletter*, X (May 1969), p. 63.

the work's satiric edge will be blunted. The technique of extrapolation demands a commitment to logic.[10]

In detailing some examples, I am going to confine myself to my third science-fiction category, in which a startling rationale is involved, because I find the third type the most significant as an expression of the philosophical sense of the apocalyptic imagination and because this category has not previously been isolated by critics of the genre. One American example is provided by H. P. Lovecraft's stories, which, oscillating uncertainly between the gothic and science fiction, are held together by a mythology that takes as its starting point the assumption that man is only the latest of a series of beings who have inhabited the Earth. Among the earlier denizens were a race who discovered the secret of time travel. Lovecraft's mythology is quite complicated in all its ramifications, but what he basically suggests is that many ghostly phenomena may be explained as the materializations of Earth's early time travelers. I shall have more to say about Lovecraft toward the conclusion of this study. The same goes for another American writer, Kurt Vonnegut, Jr., who, in *The Sirens of Titan* (1959), tells us that eons ago a spaceship containing a robotlike alien crash-landed on one of the moons of Saturn. It turns out that the history of humanity has been manipulated by related aliens from a distant galaxy, in order to allow for that time when a spaceship from Earth reaches Titan "accidentally" carrying a piece of material that will function as a spare part! Arthur C. Clarke provides an English example of this species of science fiction in *2001: A Space Odyssey* (1968). It is speculated that we owe our present stage of evolution to the interference of spiritual beings while we were at the ape stage. But for the appearance of the mysterious slab, the human race would have died out in its infancy. The result of entertaining these revolutionary notions is the sensation, however momentary, of a philosophical apocalypse.

[10] The plausibility issue points to an important distinction between science fiction and fantasy, hinging on what Delany calls the "level of subjunctivity," ibid., pp. 61–64. H. Bruce Franklin distinguishes between types of fiction on a similar basis in *Future Perfect: American Science Fiction of the Nineteenth Century* (New York, 1966), p. 3. The lack of a plausible relationship between fantasy and the "real world" makes it impossible to speak about works of fantasy effecting a philosophical apocalypse.

II

I want now to suggest that certain characteristics of science fiction, particularly the philosophical apocalyptic kind, are present in American literature generally and, secondly, try to explain why. H. Bruce Franklin has done much of the groundwork in preparing his anthology *Future Perfect: American Science Fiction of the Nineteenth Century*. He concludes: "There was no major nineteenth-century American writer of fiction, and indeed few in the second rank, who did not write some science fiction or at least one utopian romance." "Rip van Winkle," he notes, "is a time-travel story," while other examples include Cooper's *The Monikins* (1835) and *The Crater* (1848), Melville's *Mardi*, Twain's *A Connecticut Yankee in King Arthur's Court*, and (less convincingly) Stephen Crane's *The Monster*.[11] The inclusion of the allegorical Hawthorne is also questionable, but Poe, Fitz-James O'Brien, Edward Bellamy, and Ambrose Bierce consistently wrote science fiction. It is only necessary to think of the affinity between Melville's Ahab and Jules Verne's Nemo and the degree to which *2001: A Space Odyssey* is indebted to *Moby-Dick* (particularly in basing metaphysical speculation on technology) to recognize the science-fictional element operational in the latter work.[12]

To speak more generally, characterization is generally slighted in American fiction in favor of the expression of ideas and metaphysical abstractions. The same bias is true of science fiction. A concern for the meaning of existence invariably reaches its limits with an awareness of cyclical process. In this connection it is interesting to relate the cyclical patterning of many science-fiction stories, typified perhaps by H. G. Wells' *The Time Machine*, to such American works as Irving's "Rip Van Winkle," Thoreau's *Walden*, Fitzgerald's *The Great Gatsby*, and Hemingway's *The Sun Also Rises*, in which cyclical theory is particularly pertinent. The fact that much "space opera" science fiction is a displaced form of the "Western" is indisputable,

[11] Franklin, op. cit., p. x.

[12] Note also that Ray Bradbury wrote the script for the latest film version of *Moby-Dick* and the existence of Philip José Farmer's science-fiction sequel, *The Wind Whales of Ishmael* (New York, 1971).

but there is also some relationship between the mystical impulse of science fiction and American transcendentalism. Furthermore, like much science fiction, American literature is notable for its prophetic character, perhaps attributable to the American impetus toward originality: sophisticated symbolic techniques in the novel, and experimental methodology in poetry, developed in America long before they became standardized in Europe. The sharp juxtaposition in American literature, noted previously, of pragmatism and materialism with the transcendental and speculative is implicit in the term science fiction and suggests something about the paradoxical nature of the genre that is lost in terms like "speculative fiction" or "speculative fabulation." [13]

Then there is the quality of wonder, which Tony Tanner, in *The Reign of Wonder* (1965), finds in American literature. However, it is even more characteristic of science fiction, as is apparent from the title of Damon Knight's book on the subject, *In Search of Wonder* (1967). Delany talks about a "sense of wonder" and "these violet nets of wonder called speculative fiction." [14] And as an epigraph to *The Martian Chronicles* (1950), Ray Bradbury has these lines: " 'It is good to renew one's sense of wonder,' said the philosopher. 'Space travel has again made children of us all.' "

III

The question remains: why should many of the characteristics of science fiction be in alignment with many of the features that distinguish American literature? In large measure, the answer lies in the fact that science fiction derives from the romance, which, thanks largely to Richard Chase, we now recognize as the basic form of the American novel. [15] Works that we call science fiction

[13] I would speculate that dissatisfaction with the term science fiction is less a reflection of doubt concerning its descriptive appropriateness than the result of a desire to disassociate from that body of literature called science fiction the aura of opprobrium frequently engendered by the term. Note that science-fiction works of obvious literary merit, such as *Brave New World* and *1984* are not generally thought of as science fiction.

[14] Op. cit., p. 63.

[15] See *The American Novel and Its Tradition* (New York, 1957).

were originally called "scientific romances." Actually all popular escapist literature—the gothic horror story, romantic fiction, the Western, detective and thriller fiction, pornography and science fiction—derives from the romance, and given the prevalence of the romance in American literature, it is not surprising that all forms of the popularized romance have flourished with particular intensity in America. Both Fiedler and Harry Levin have argued that it is the gothic offshoot of the romance that best expresses the American imagination.[16] No one, to my knowledge, has examined in detail the extent to which science fiction has functioned as an outlet for the American writer, although Fiedler, in defining science fiction as a neogothic form, includes it in his thesis.

If biblical myth has provided American writers with a way of ordering their subject matter, the romance, particularly the gothic *and* science-fictional offshoots, has provided the characteristic mode. My point is that most of the reasons adduced by Chase to explain the prominence of the romance—in particular its latitude, its being in Hawthorne's terms "a neutral territory, somewhere between the real world and fairy-land," and its suitability as an expression of the incongruity of the American situation—also explain the existence of science fiction and science-fictional elements in American literature.[17]

But there are other factors, which relate specifically to science fiction. To some degree, surely, the lack of a usable past must have encouraged American writers to look to the future for their myths. After all, America has always been a land of promises. Indeed America, with its surrealistic skyscrapers, provides one alternative blueprint of the future for the rest of the world. The notion of the American Adam is common enough. Less common is the recognition that the idea of a second Adam, or a second Eve for that

[16] See Harry Levin, *The Power of Blackness* (New York, 1958), and Leslie A. Fiedler, *Love and Death in the American Novel* (New York, 1960). Fiedler considers science fiction only in the revised edition (1967), pp. 500, 502. Certainly the evasion of heterosexual relationships, which Fiedler observes in American literature, is also notable in science fiction, which is generally characterized by an extreme purity of subject matter—unless, of course, one wants to see science fiction as disguising fantasies of a return to the womb!

[17] *The Centenary Edition of the Works of Nathaniel Hawthorne* (Columbus, Ohio, 1962), p. 36.

matter, is generally the province of science fiction. What usually happens is that, after the nuclear holocaust, two survivors see themselves as the progenitors of a new world.[18] "Utopias" and dystopias are regular science-fiction fodder, and, as A. N. Kaul argues in *The American Vision* (1963), fodder for the American imagination, which is obsessed with dreams of a utopia. American society is, in fact, a projected utopia that now seems to have turned into a dystopia. Note also that the area beyond the frontier and the Indian once represented that unknown and alien exotic so beloved of science fiction. In a sense, the exploration of space has supplied America with a further outlet for its tradition of frontiersmanship. America's fall from grace, Leo Marx suggests in *The Machine in the Garden*, may have something to do with the industrial revolution and the growth of technology.[19] And, as the term science fiction implies, to some people it has seemed that the genre derives its subject matter from scientific advances. Certainly science fiction flourished in the throes of the industrial revolution. But the tremendous contemporaneous influence of Charles Darwin should also be appreciated, both upon "mainstream" American literature and also upon the opening up of a temporal and cyclical canvas directly amenable only to science fiction.

In general terms, the proliferation of science fiction is a response to abruptly changing social conditions. During times of stability, when change neither happens nor is expected, or happens so gradually as to be barely noticeable, writers are unlikely to spend time describing the future condition of society, because there is no reason to expect any significant difference. With the nineteenth century, things speeded up, and now change is a constant and unnerving factor in our daily lives. If we are to live rationally, and not just for the moment, some attempt must be made to anticipate

[18] See, for example, my concluding remarks on Ray Bradbury's *The Martian Chronicles* in the next chapter.

[19] See *The Machine in the Garden: Technology and the Pastoral Ideal in America* (Fair Lawn, N.J., 1964). Incidentally, it is interesting to note that, in *The Tempest*, which Marx relates to the pastoral attraction of North America (pp. 35–72), Kingsley Amis finds science-fictional prototypes: scientist and attractive daughter, "an early mutant" in the shape of Caliban, while Ariel functions as an "anthropomorphised mobile scanner" (*New Maps of Hell*, p. 30). Can we then speak of *The Tempest* as a science-fiction vision of America?

future situations. Hence writers are drawn to science fiction; it is an outgrowth and an expression of crisis. Thus Robert Heinlein attests to the value of science fiction: "We cannot drive safely by looking only in the rear-view mirror [shades of McLuhan]; it is more urgent to watch the road ahead." [20] The analogy is imperfect, but Heinlein's point is sound enough, although science fiction is not primarily valuable as prediction. Rather, it teaches adaptability and elasticity of mind in the face of change.

A final and most important explanation of the science-fictional elements in American literature is the realization that the discovery and colonization of America are imaginatively equivalent to the conquest of space and the future colonization of, say, the moon or Mars. Since the colonization of other worlds belongs to the realm of science fiction, one might indeed expect to discover that certain aspects of American literature have something in common with science fiction. The essential element that they have in common, I see as the apocalyptic imagination.

[20] See *The Science Fiction Novel*, ed. by Basil Davenport (Chicago, 1959), p. 54. ···

Science Fiction and the Future

by John Huntington

From the very beginning of modern SF, enthusiasts, apparently unsatisfied with the mere popularity of the form, perceiving that at some level it does more than simply give pleasure, have asserted that SF serves an important educational purpose: by engaging us in the act of imagining the unknown (they tell us) SF prepares us for the future. William Rupp takes it as a "favorable sign" that 48 percent of a sampling of English professors defined SF as "a type of story that ... tries to anticipate the impact of future technological developments on society." Some recent guides to the future go so far as to insist that anyone who expects to cope with the future at all must read SF. "Science fiction should be required reading for Future I," declares Alvin Toffler. Arthur C. Clarke maintains that "A critical ... reading of science fiction is essential training for anyone wishing to look more than ten years ahead." [1] Though these "futurologists" refrain from claiming the kind of literal prophesy popular with SF apologists thirty years ago, they nevertheless agree with the earlier defenders in believing that SF trains its readers to anticipate the unexpected and helps them to encounter change and a future that will certainly differ radically from the present.

There is, to be sure, a genuine intellectual pleasure to be derived from imagining in the fullest detail possible a previously unknown or unthought-of machine, society, race, or environment, but this pleasure probably does not have the educational value that is

[1] Rupp, "Science-Fiction and the Literary Community," *Riverside Quarterly*, 5 (1972), 210–11. Toffler, *Future Shock* (1970: rpt. New York: Bantam, 1971), p. 425. Clarke, *Profiles of the Future* (1963: rpt. New York: Bantam, 1964), p. xiii.

claimed for it. Though SF often gives us a *sense* of facing the unknown, its true insights are generally into the known, and its primary value lies not in its ability to train us for the future but in its ability to engage a particular set of problems to which science itself gives rise and which belong, not to the future, but to the present. At its core SF is a powerfully conventional and deeply conservative—though not necessarily right-wing—form of literature which, rather than assaulting the unknown by bold risks of the imagination, tames the threat of the future and in doing so articulates one aspect of our present human situation in a way no other literary form can. In asserting that SF does not open up the future in the way its defenders wish it did, I may seem to be merely repeating what the debunkers of such literature have always claimed. The debunkers, of course, have not been entirely without truth. Where they have gone astray is in thinking that since SF is not what some of its loudest touters say, it is a cheap fraud. On the contrary, though one regrets that SF is not always all that it might be, one can perceive a value in even the mediocre hack work. My concern, therefore, is not to disavow typical SF, but to reinterpret its function.

By "typical SF" I mean SF of the sort published in the United States in the 1930s, forties, and fifties, the product of what is now called, either fondly or scornfully, "The Golden Age of SF." I am, therefore, excluding from specific consideration some good SF written in the past fifteen years which, however much it may fit in with some of what I am saying, makes a point of breaking with the traditions and conventions that flourished earlier. The idea of science in this recent SF is much looser than that which dominates the earlier work, and many of the new writers have even rebelled against the name "science fiction" itself in favor of the broader and less restrictive title of "speculative fiction." Typical SF, however, constitutes a coherent and narrow genre with some quite rigorous boundaries. In order to understand its value we need to begin by considering what it means to claim to treat "science" in fiction. Then we can go on to consider how and why powerful and often clichéd literary conventions hold the firm place they do in a form which brags of its freedom from "old ways of thought." Finally, we can examine why this supposedly future-oriented fiction must be conservative if it is going to remain true to its scientific premises. Again let me stress that my aim is not to attack SF. It seems to me that the conservative activity that most SF engages in is in fact more valuable than the "mind-expanding" activity that is popularly claimed for it.

I

We must begin our considerations with the fact of addiction. Unlike the generally literate reader who occasionally and selectively reads a work classified on the cover as SF and who evaluates what he has read according to a scale of fairly well formulated, well understood, and widely accepted values, the SF addict is indiscriminate and seems to satisfy his craving simply by being in the world of SF. The SF addict is not a connoisseur; he may have favorite authors or books, but he often reads whatever SF he can get his hands on. He has expectations that drive him, and he gains satisfactions from the experience of a wide variety of quite forgettable stories. In reading SF the addict participates in a world in which the literary experience is secondary to some larger pleasure.

As to what it is that particularly attracts the addict, it is important to note that, though fancy machines abound in SF, the mere presence of yet-unknown technology does not satisfy his craving. While clichés such as ray-guns somehow hold him in thrall, the ingenious machines that make islands fly in Book III of *Gulliver's Travels* bore him. The reason is, I suggest, that the addict is interested not only in exercising his ingenuity, but also in trying to cope with the controlling presence of science, and Swift is simply too safe from his scientists and their productions. Though modern ideas of science are clearly present in the early part of the eighteenth century, to Swift they offer a repellent *alternative,* not a *necessary context;* they do not shape his life.

On the other hand, since it is this scientific context rather than the surface details of technology that appeals to the addict, the presence of obsolete or impossible machines need not discourage his enthusiasm. Though accurate scientific detail helps to establish the context, a "mistake" such as the ramp up Pike's Peak which launches one of Robert Heinlein's early rockets, while it may provoke a smile, does not seriously mar the story's satisfactions. As it actually functions in a story, technology is usually as magical as it is scientific. Michel Butor wisely observes that the difference between a spaceship and a flying carpet is not that we really understand one better than the other, but that the spaceship signifies a world of science.[2] Any particular technological development is an arbitrary event; its absence might change the surface shape of the world somewhat, but it would not create contradiction or confusion. The deep structure of the world, as interpreted by science itself, remains unchanged in spite of the random creations of the engineers.

SF answers a craving, not for a new and plausible technology, but for a science which will mediate between a conviction of the necessity of events—that is, a strict determinism—and a belief in creative freedom. On the one hand, "the laws of physics are the decrees of fate." By investigating "the remorseless workings of things," [3] scientists understand necessity. But, on the other hand, science converts that understanding into a means for freedom, for the very regularity of nature, as revealed and interpreted by science, permits us to transcend nature's limitations through control, prediction, and invention. By understanding the law of gravity we can escape Earth. Thus, to a partial extent, science functions like religion. A "law of physics" is every bit as absolute as a "law of God," and both laws promise security and perhaps even transcendence to those who understand and obey. Unlike religion, however, science advances with man's acquiescence and contribution. The final catastrophe, formerly God's to initiate or forestall, is now man's. The problem is that we do not experience in actuality the awesome freedom that this idea of science promises. For the scientist himself, science represents, not heroic challenge and freedom, but an abstract, narrow pursuit which results in, at best, minor victories won at the cost of enormous drudgery and frustration. Even the most major individual contribution to science changes the course of things only slightly. For the nonscientist the ease of ignorance does not make any lighter the sense of inexorable destiny that science imparts. The understanding of necessity does not liberate. Science, as we experience it, oppresses.

[2] "Science Fiction: The Crisis of its Growth," trans. Richard Howard, *Partisan Review*, 34 (1967), 595.
[3] Alfred North Whitehead, *Science and the Modern World* (1925: rpt. New York: Free Press, 1967), pp. 10–11.

By means of *fiction* SF restores to the myth of science the promise of freedom and control that experience fails to give it. Whereas science deals with necessities, fiction offers freedoms. Whereas science explores and explains what absolutely must happen, fiction creates its own sequences and consequences. The paradox of the name, "science fiction," encompasses, therefore, a wide range of fiction that, while ostensibly treating of the inevitable, offers fancy. This paradox is, I suggest, in itself, an important source of pleasure for the addict. He can read and sincerely enjoy stories that engage this paradox even though by conventional literary standards they are worthy of contempt. He enjoys on a level other than that to which the usual critical questions probe.

Whereas conventional fiction is bound by the laws of the probable, SF, though its *subject* is just that reality that binds normal fiction, is free from that bond. Paradoxically, SF is one of the least scientific of fictions because it owes hardly anything to the facts of experience. Unlike conventional fiction, which accepts the necessities of experience as given and fantasizes from there, SF sets up fictional necessities and then obeys them. SF closely resembles pure fantasy in that it escapes nature's rules and makes its own. SF addicts, however, insist that there is an important difference between SF and fantasy. What seems to pacify the SF addict is the bow to science, even if it is a mere gesture, that SF makes, and what disturbs him about fantasy is that it acknowledges no law that prevents the freedom of imagination from seeming arbitrary. The SF addict wants to feel the tension of the paradox of freedom within a structured imperative. It may be the desire for this paradox that accounts for the repeated attempts of writers and readers of SF to define prescriptive rules for the genre.

Though the surface message of a novel or story may assert a simple ideology, the paradox of science as a liberating understanding of necessity still functions at a deep level in SF. Optimistic SF, which (while promulgating a view of the easy freedom science will bring) often exults in brute power and totalitarian control, might seem to deny the element of freedom in the paradox. As fiction about science, however, it still engages the whole paradox even as its surface vulgarizes and trivializes it. In a similar way, pessimistic SF, by attacking science as simply oppressive, on its surface limits the range of the paradox, but in its deeper form reasserts it. The two ideological poles of SF differ in what public attitudes they engage: pessimistic SF appeals to the audience's anxieties about science, optimistic to its audience's hopes for science. But they still share a deep structure that unites in some way scientific necessity and imaginative freedom.

II

Given the paradox that lies at the heart of SF and the importance of the freedom represented by fiction, it may seem inconsistent that the genre, which one might expect to explore the possibilities of fictional styles and forms, has traditionally conformed closely to a clear and powerful set of stylistic and narrative conventions. To a certain extent the conventionality of much SF can be attributed to the narrow views of the editors of the pulp magazines that dominated the field in its early years of popularity. John W. Campbell, the very influential editor of *Astounding*, advised writers that the ending of a story "must solve the problems directly raised in the story—and do it succinctly. Quick and sharp." [4] No wonder, given such a narrow conception of fictional form, that punch-line stories abound in the SF of the "Golden Age." But since many addicts seem to get more pleasure from conventional work than from experimental work, we may suspect that, far from being an obstruction to the addicts' enjoyment, the conventions that grow out of such dogmas as Campbell's actually add to the appeal of the form.

We must distinguish the inherent consequences of the form from the conventions. The former develop naturally from the importance of science to the genre and entail an emphasis on idea and a de-emphasis on character. The conventions, however, are purely literary; they derive from the experience of works of SF rather than from any intrinsic quality of science or of fiction. On the most obvious level, the conventions consist of a group of plots and situations that are frequently repeated, and one can easily understand why most of them are popular. More important for our

[4] "The Science of Science Fiction Writing," in *Of Worlds Beyond*, ed. Lloyd Arthur Eshbach (Chicago: Advent, 1947), p. 100.

purposes are the conventions that the form has taken on for no apparent reason, the gratuitous insignia that mark a story as hard-core SF and to which an addict immediately responds. The most powerful of these arbitrary and self-chosen conventions are a limited and stereotyped cast of characters and a limited set of languages.

Conventions offer the security of the recognizable and thereby cushion the impact of any new idea, of anything unknown. The addict, therefore, usually experiences a new idea gradually rather than suddenly; he begins a story by settling into the known world of SF and then discovering what is new here. The nonaddict doesn't experience this gradual, at times quite subtle, development of the new idea; for him the very conventions are unknown, and he may get the impression that SF is more daring than it actually is. On the other hand, the mechanical way the conventions are often invoked will probably offend the newcomer more than the addict, for the newcomer will see only the awkwardness and not experience the consolations that compensate the addict.

Once the field of convention is strong enough, the skillful writer can create the feeling of the unknown simply by breaking the convention. The powerful aura of mystery at the end of Clarke's *Childhood's End* owes much to the solid conventionality of the first half of the novel. The addict's sense of confusion and new understanding in the last parts of the novel is caused in large part by the collapse of the conventions originally invoked and the discovery of a new set. Whether or not one actually conceives anything new in *Childhood's End*, one gets a sense of *what it is like* to comprehend a reality and a mind beyond the range of normal human perception and thought.

SF that relies strongly on conventions may justly be termed conservative, for the conventions, whatever their virtues, impose limitations on the imagination. They define the areas in which the unknown can appear and delimit the restructuring of reality that can take place. Those who attack SF often seize on this aspect to justify their scorn, but the addict is not being simply unimaginative when he engages in this convention-bound activity. In fact, insofar as the addict takes pleasure in exploring the "unknown" in the context of the "known," that is within the frame defined by the conventions, he is recapitulating in significant ways the activity of normal scientists. Science itself, in the formulation of Thomas S.

Kuhn,[5] is a tradition-bound activity; the normal scientist does not discover new realms of knowledge; he solves puzzles that are defined by the "paradigm" that the reigning theories postulate. In solving such a puzzle a scientist makes a previously unaccounted-for event conform to the dominant theory. A scientific "revolution" involves constructing a new paradigm; it takes place only when the old paradigm proves itself incapable of explaining the observations it engenders. Like the scientist who works within a paradigm and depends on it for his questions and his goals, the SF addict has a paradigm which consists of the conventions of the form, and he knows how to discover pleasure in the puzzles that the conventions allow. Like a good paradigm, a strong convention tells the reader where to look, how to look, and what to look for, and, as in the situation of the normal scientist, the rewards are not new structures by which to organize experience or understanding, but a reinforcement of the paradigm or of the conventions. The SF addict is a "puzzle-solver" just as the normal scientist is; like that scientist, the addict does not really discover new frameworks; he exhibits and enjoys his mastery over what he already knows.

"Normal science" can, of course, become stultifying; similarly, in SF the conventions can easily become simply and only a limitation that insures that no truly imaginative or creative act will occur. Not all conventional SF is so complacent, however. When it is stimulated by constant contact with new ideas, the conventional becomes an expanding context that develops with each new work in the form and which gradually grows into increasingly accurate and subtle modes of depicting realities. But, even at its most lively, the convention always defines limits which SF cannot completely abandon without losing much of the real pleasure and attraction it has for the addict. The conventions anchor SF, give it a form of believability, though the dependable aspect that the SF addict recognizes and trusts is not a semblance to a known physical reality as in ordinary fiction, but a set of purely literary mannerisms. The conventions stamp a work as SF and thereby assure the addict that his habit will be satisfied. And like the tensions in the concept of "science fiction" itself, the play of literary convention against

---

[5] *The Structure of Scientific Revolutions*, 2nd ed., enlarged (Chicago: University of Chicago Press, 1970).

scientific ingenuity generates a paradox whose pressures the addict finds pleasurable.

III

The conservatism of SF, which we have likened to that of normal science, is easily confused with *political* conservatism, a connection encouraged by the politics of some of the main writers of SF. In an essay in *Ramparts* on the politics of SF, Richard Lupoff suggests as a general rule that those writers who are optimistic about the possibilities of science tend to be right-wing and that those pessimistic about science's possibilities tend to be left-wing. Again, the strong influence of John W. Campbell, optimistic about science and politically conservative, may be partly responsible. But Lupoff derives the dichotomy from something more essential, something inherent in a mode of thought. "Whatever else divides these traditionalists," he argues, "they are united by their engineering mentality and its preference for violent, repressive solutions to the political problems posed in its novels. These people seem convinced that the application of the right materials and the right forces will solve any problem. It is obvious in their fiction." This same "engineering mentality," Lupoff claims, leads to fiction that "by virtue of its dedication to control, to predictability, to the finite, closed-end solution" is unable to cope with humans, only with machines.[6] The word *engineer* does a lot of hard work here, not all of it respectable. Also, though Lupoff's theory is clearly accurate if applied to a select group of SF writers, and though his criticism of these writers is well taken, the generalization does not stand up. To use his own test of political position (the attitude expressed towards the Vietnam war in ads in *If* magazine in 1967) a number of writers clearly belonging to the optimistic, "engineering mentality" turn out to be left-wing. The optimism about science and the political conservatism of much SF do not seem to be functionally related.

There is, however, an element of conservatism, not political, which is inescapable for those SF writers who make any claim to deal in what they would call a "responsible" way with the future

[6] "Science Fiction Hawks and Doves: Whose Future Will You Buy?" *Ramparts*, (February 1972), p. 27.

and which intrudes even in their most grandiose and far-fetched visions. Whether the aim is to explore fictional possibilities or actually to prophesy, extrapolation is inherently a conservative imaginative act. If we in the present are going to think about the future in any *scientific* way, we have to reason from the experience of the past. For the future to be knowable there must be some pattern of continuity, some universal process, whether of change or of stagnation, which we have already perceived and which allows us to extrapolate to what will be. This process of looking ahead, as the writers themselves insist, is not visionary; its "scientific" basis, however, dooms it to be conservative, for in one way or another it must enforce some pattern from the past on the future.

No matter how "scientific" their basis, all visions of the future that foresee future discoveries are fictions.[7] Thus, again, in SF's claim to treat the future scientifically we meet the paradoxical conjunction of science and fiction, of determinism and freedom, which is an important source of pleasure and interest for the SF addict. The paradox at the heart of "extrapolation" is evident in a statement of Isaac Asimov's defending the process: "it is legitimate to extrapolate from the past because sometimes such extrapolations are fairly close to what happens."[8] On the one hand, in claiming that extrapolation is "legitimate," Asimov implies a rigorous and knowable relation between past and future, while on the other hand, in the qualifications *sometimes* and *fairly close,* he betrays the actual flimsiness of the logical necessity linking them. Though his statement really allows for any kind of fantasy, it invokes the conservative method of reasoning from the past to sanction the imaginative act.

One may reasonably ask whether it is possible to imagine or describe any future that is not in some way based on the past; the wildest fantasy, after all, if it is to be comprehensible, must at some point anchor itself in the known. But popular SF, rather than pushing towards the bounds of the truly unexplored, tends to be more imaginatively conservative than even its "scientific" method

[7] See Karl R. Popper, *The Poverty of Historicism,* 3rd ed. (1961: rpt. New York: Harper Torchbook, 1964), p. vii et passim.

[8] "Social Science Fiction," in *Modern Science Fiction,* ed. Reginald Bretnor (New York: Coward-McCann, 1953), p. 183.

requires. In this respect writers as politically different as Ray Bradbury and Robert Heinlein share a similar conservatism in that they both look to the familiar past for their exotic futures. In *The Martian Chronicles* Bradbury frequently describes the future on Mars in terms of the midwest in the 1920s. In "The Roads Must Roll" Heinlein models his transport workers on the U. S. Marines. And just as institutions and images from the actual past shape the SF writers' visions of the future, the overwhelming conventionality of this form of literature makes it almost inevitable that styles, images, and figures from past literature will also dominate the futures described. Thus, the presence of kings and dukes in SF novels is less a sign of a feudal political inclination inherent in the engineering mentality than an instance of the inevitable persistence of traditional literary forms and figures in SF. This conservative prospect, in which the future is a superficial transformation of a familiar past and described in familiar terms, characterizes almost all popular SF. If SF gives the impression of facing the unknown future with daring and foresight, it is seldom because it really imagines a new future in any radical way, or because it forecasts change with any certainty or precision, but because, by relying on traditional literary conventions and forms, and by repeating historical and psychological patterns from the past, it manages to domesticate the future, to render it habitable and, in spite of a somewhat strange surface, basically familiar.

That it does not help us understand and cope with the future in the ways its apologists claim does not mean that the genre fails, however. Like other forms of literature, SF treats the present, not the future. It differs from other forms in that it engages science, not as a tangential aspect of human affairs, but as a central phenomenon, and as a genre it establishes a context within which the addict can experience the liberating paradox of freedom and necessity that science presents. At the deepest level, therefore, the addict draws his important satisfaction from his knowledge of the genre itself; he trusts it, and he appreciates individual works, not so much for their ingenuity, originality, or foresight, but for the way they recognizably reinforce his sense of the genre. For this pleasure he can overlook many literary faults. That is why SF can be very popular and important and yet have few, if any, works that are acknowledged as "classics" by anyone outside of the circle of addicts itself.

Chronology of Important Dates

1926–36   *Amazing Stories* founded by Hugo Gernsback (1926); E. E. Smith, *The Skylark of Space* (1928); *Astounding Stories* founded (1930); W. Olaf Stapledon, *Last and First Men* (1930); Aldous Huxley, *Brave New World* (1932)

Stock market crash, beginning of Great Depression (1929); Franklin Roosevelt elected president (1932); Adolf Hitler achieves power in Germany (1933)

1937–45   John W. Campbell, Jr. becomes editor of *Astounding Stories* (1937); C. S. Lewis, *Out of the Silent Planet* (1938); Robert A. Heinlein, "Future History" series begun in *Astounding* with "Lifeline" (1939); Isaac Asimov, "Foundation" series begun in *Astounding* (1942); A. E. van Vogt, *The World of Null-A* (1945)

World War II (1939–45); commercial television (1939); United Nations charter (1945); atomic bomb dropped on Hiroshima, Japan (1945)

1946–55   George Orwell, *1984* (1947); *Magazine of Fantasy and Science Fiction* founded (1949); Ray Bradbury, *The Martian Chronicles* (1950); *Galaxy Science Fiction* founded (1950); Alfred Bester, *The Demolished Man* (1953); Arthur C. Clarke, *Childhood's End* (1953); Theodore Sturgeon, *More Than Human* (1953); Frederick Pohl and C. M. Kornbluth, *The Space Merchants* (1953)

Transistor developed (1947); People's Republic of China established (1949); Korean War (1950–53); hydrogen bomb exploded (1952); death of Stalin (1953); structure of DNA molecule explained (1953)

1956–63   Ivan Yefremov, *Andromeda* (1957); Walter M. Miller, Jr., *A Canticle for Leibowitz* (1959); Kurt Vonnegut, *The Sirens of Titan* (1959); Stanislaw Lem, *Solaris* (1961); Philip K. Dick, *The Man in the High Castle* (1962); J. G. Ballard, *The Drowned World* (1963)

Sputnik I, first artificial satellite (1957); Yuri Gagarin, first man in orbit (1961); Cuban missile crisis (1962); John F. Kennedy assassinated (1963)

1964-74   Frank Herbert, *Dune* (1965); *Dangerous Visions*, edited by Harlan Ellison (1967); Stanley Kubrick and Arthur Clarke, *2001: A Space Odyssey* (1968); Ursula K. LeGuin, *The Left Hand of Darkness* (1969), *The Dispossessed* (1974)

U. S. actively engaged in Vietnam (1964-73); first heart transplant (1967); Neil Armstrong, first man on moon (1969); resignation of Richard M. Nixon (1974)

Notes on the Editor and Contributors

MARK ROSE, the editor of this volume, is Professor of English at the University of Illinois, Urbana-Champaign. He is the author of a novel, *Golding's Tale*, as well as scholarly studies of Renaissance literature: *Heroic Love, Shakespearean Design*, and *Spenser's Art*. He is also editor of *Twentieth Century Interpretations of Antony and Cleopatra*.

KINGSLEY AMIS, the English novelist, is the author of *Lucky Jim, Take a Girl Like You, One Fat Englishman, The Green Man*, and many other books. Together with Robert Conquest he edits an annual anthology of science fiction.

ROBERT CONQUEST, who spent many years in the British Foreign Service, writes principally on contemporary Russian history and politics. He also publishes poetry, fiction, and literary criticism.

MICHAEL HOLQUIST has published essays on Lewis Carroll's nonsense and the metaphysical detective story as well as on topics in Russian literature. Currently writing a book on Dostoevski, he is chairman of the Slavic Literature Department, University of Texas, Austin.

JOHN HUNTINGTON has taught courses in science fiction at Rutgers University and the University of Rhode Island and has published essays on science fiction and on Renaissance poetry. He is presently working on a study of H. G. Wells.

DAVID KETTERER is Associate Professor of English, Concordia University, Montreal. He writes on American literature and on science fiction.

STANISLAW LEM, a Polish writer who was originally trained in medicine, has published books on the history and philosophy of science as well as literary criticism and such science fiction as *Solaris, The Invincible*, and *The Cyberiad*. Most of his work has not yet been translated into English.

C. S. LEWIS, who died in 1963, was Professor of Medieval and Renaissance English at Cambridge University. His scholarly works include *The Allegory of Love* and the volume on nondramatic literature of the sixteenth century in the *Oxford History of English Literature*. He also wrote children's books, religious treatises, and three science-fiction novels: *Out of the Silent Planet, Perelandra*, and *That Hideous Strength*.

ERIC RABKIN is Associate Professor of English at the University of Michigan, where he teaches courses on fantasy and on science fiction. He is the author of *Narrative Suspense* and is currently writing a book on science fiction in collaboration with Robert Scholes.

ROBERT SCHOLES, Professor of English and Comparative Literature, Brown University, is widely known for such books as *The Nature of Narrative* (written together with Robert Kellogg), *The Fabulators*, and *Structuralism in Literature*.

SUSAN SONTAG is best known as a critic for *Against Interpretation*, but she is also a novelist, a film-maker, and a contributor to such periodicals as *Partisan Review* and *Commentary*.

DARKO SUVIN, Associate Professor of English, McGill University, was born and educated at Zagreb, Yugoslavia. He has lectured and published widely on drama as well as on science fiction and is co-editor of *Science-Fiction Studies*.

Selected Bibliography

Brian W. Aldiss. *Billion Year Spree: The True History of Science Fiction.* Garden City, N. Y.: Doubleday, 1973. The best history of the genre to date.

Kingsley Amis. *New Maps of Hell: A Survey of Science Fiction.* New York: Harcourt, Brace, and World, 1960. Classic introductory discussion.

William Atheling, Jr. (James Blish). *The Issue at Hand.* Chicago: Advent, 1964. Essays by one of the best science-fiction writer-critics.

————. *More Issues at Hand.* Chicago: Advent, 1972.

J. O. Bailey. *Pilgrims Through Space and Time: Trends and Patterns in Scientific and Utopian Fiction.* New York: Argus Books, 1947. Pioneering survey of early science fiction.

Bernard Bergonzi. *The Early H. G. Wells: A Study of the Scientific Romances.* Manchester: Manchester University Press, 1961. Classic study of Wells's science fiction.

Reginald Bretnor, ed. *Modern Science Fiction: Its Meaning and Its Future.* New York: Coward-McCann, 1953. Essays by science-fiction writers and editors.

————. *Science Fiction, Today and Tomorrow.* New York: Harper and Row, 1974. Essays by science-fiction writers and editors.

Thomas D. Clareson, ed. *SF: The Other Side of Realism.* Bowling Green, Ohio: Bowling Green University Popular Press, 1971. Good collection of critical essays.

————. *Science Fiction Criticism: An Annotated Checklist.* Kent, Ohio: Kent State University Press, 1972. Invaluable.

I. F. Clarke. *Voices Prophesying War, 1763–1984.* New York: Oxford University Press, 1966. The "future war" theme.

Robert C. Elliott. *The Shape of Utopia: Studies in a Literary Genre.* Chicago: University of Chicago Press, 1970.

H. Bruce Franklin. *Future Perfect: American Science Fiction of the Nineteenth Century.* New York: Oxford University Press, 1966. Anthology of fiction with important introductory material.

James Gunn. *Alternate Worlds: The Illustrated History of Science Fiction.* Englewood Cliffs, N. J.: Prentice-Hall, Inc., 1975. Complements Aldiss's history.

Mark R. Hillegas. *The Future as Nightmare: H. G. Wells and the Anti-Utopians.* New York: Oxford University Press, 1967. The dystopian tradition.

David Ketterer. *New Worlds for Old: The Apocalyptic Imagination, Science Fiction, and American Literature.* Bloomington: Indiana University Press, 1974. Important study.

Damon Knight. *In Search of Wonder.* Chicago: Advent, 1967. Essays by one of the best science-fiction writer-critics.

Stanislaw Lem. *Fantastyka i futurologia.* Cracow, Poland: Wydawnictwo Literackie, 1970. Science fiction and futurology.

Sam Moskowitz. *Explorers of the Infinite: Shapers of Science Fiction.* Cleveland: World, 1963. Biographical studies.

―――. *Seekers of Tomorrow: Masters of Modern Science Fiction.* Cleveland, 1966. Biographical studies.

Marjorie Hope Nicolson. *Voyages to the Moon.* New York: Macmillan, 1948. The early moon-voyage stories.

Robert M. Philmus. *Into the Unknown: The Evolution of Science Fiction from Francis Godwin to H. G. Wells.* Berkeley: University of California Press, 1970.

Robert Scholes. *Structural Fabulation: An Essay on Fiction of the Future.* Notre Dame: University of Notre Dame Press, 1975. Provocative introductory discussions.

There are two outstanding journals devoted to critical discussion of science fiction: *Extrapolation*, the journal of the Modern Language Association Seminar on Science Fiction, edited by Thomas D. Clareson, and *Science-Fiction Studies*, edited by R. D. Mullen and Darko Suvin.

TWENTIETH CENTURY VIEWS

British Authors

(continued on next page)

TWENTIETH CENTURY VIEWS

American Authors

(*continued on next page*)

(continued from previous page)